*With th
to a g...
neighbor*

Where the Great Wall Ends:
A China Memoir

Jinny Batterson

FROG & TURTLE PUBLISHING

CARY, NC

Library of Congress Cataloging-in-Publication Data
copyright registration TXu 2-075-601

ISBN 978-1-7320474-1-9

Frog and Turtle books may be purchased for educational, business or promotional use. For information please contact Jinny Batterson.

Book Design by Melinda Fine
Author photo by Jim Batterson

In loving memory of my mom,

Helen Voris,

who urged me to write and who taught me to enjoy music.

And of my dad, Calvin Voris,

who urged me to ask questions and who taught me to

value the natural world.

Contents

Introduction

"I'm finally going to see the Great Wall!" I told myself as our tour bus headed northwest out of Beijing in the summer of 1980.

Like the earliest astronauts who had hurtled into space during the 1960s and 1970s, I'd absorbed the legend that the Great Wall is one of the few man-made structures visible from space. I doubted I'd ever get to outer space, but now I was going to have my own chance to see the wall, up close and personal. What visit to China could be complete without a visit to the Great Wall?

It's been nearly forty years since that day. China was in the process of reopening to the West after a period of tension and instability. On this mid-July morning, our group's tour bus traveled along a paved road with very little automobile traffic. We shared the route mostly with other tour buses and with trucks hauling goods to Beijing. It was dry out. The wind swirled an occasional dust devil past us. Our two tour guides prepared us for our visit by taking turns reading from an English-language college text choosing several passages about this world famous landmark. Along the steeper grades, their microphone-amplified voices contended with the sounds of the gear shift and the rasp of the struggling air conditioning. Looking out the window, I'd see an occasional horse or donkey cart clip-clopping along beside the motorized traffic. Once in a while, a long, black sedan swooped past us, signaling the passage of some government official.

The restored wall portion our group got to see was hilly, several miles in all. We had about an hour for a round trip on foot—as far and as high as our lungs and muscles would allow, and still get us back to the bus in time for our departure to the next must-see sight.

I wasn't the furthest wall walker by far, but I did ascend high enough to see extended stretches of wall snaking along the crest of a ridge. About a mile away in one direction, the reconstructed portion of the wall gave way to stonework guard towers and parapets that were slightly crumbling in places. During my descent, I stopped to look more closely at some scratched-in Chinese characters that I guessed were the Chinese equivalent of "Kilroy was here" graffiti.

A young Chinese guy approached me.

"Hello," he said in English. "Where are you from?"

A little surprised to be greeted and to hear English from a Chinese, I took a moment to switch into tourist English mode. "I'm from America," I said slowly and carefully. "I'm part of a tour group that has come to see the Great Wall. It's unlike anything in the United States."

"Yes," he said. "A great accomplishment."

After a slight pause, he continued. "What is your name?" After I told him he said, "My name is Mr. Wang, and this is my colleague Mr. Liu."

The young man then explained that he and his companion were minor factory officials visiting Beijing from Shanghai. They too had not previously seen the Great Wall. He was thirty years old. He was eager for a chance to practice his English with a native speaker. His formal education had been interrupted before he completed university, but he had studied language at night on his own. He wondered if I would join him and his companion for tea—they had come in an official car that was parked nearby.

I was amazed at his openness and interest in foreigners. At the same time, although I later kicked myself for blowing a good chance for an in-depth conversation, I was nervous about losing contact with our tour group, and hesitant to take myself off with two people younger and stronger than me whom I'd just met.

"I'm sorry," I told him, "but I need to rejoin our group." With that, I continued down the slightly uneven surface of this wall segment, built to be wide enough for five horses or ten soldiers to pass abreast. I navigated carefully to avoid tripping when occasional unmarked steps angled downward among the flatter gray paving stones.

The pictures I took that summer day of the wall, of other members of our group, of the two Shanghainese who'd briefly befriended me, got lost in a subsequent move. My memories of that Great Wall visit have faded a little, but I still remember the thrill of first seeing a part of this 5,500-mile wonder.

More than a generation went by before I saw the western end of the wall, near Jaiyuguan, a small city in Gansu province. This time I was on a self-guided tour on my way to a year-long teaching assignment even further west, accompanied by my husband. Using a combination of sign language, a bilingual tourist map of the area, and some basic Mandarin, we'd engaged a taxi to take us to the fort at the "First and Greatest Pass under Heaven" along a tarred, two-lane road. Our driver, a middle-aged woman, would wait for about an hour while we toured, then return us to our basic hotel in town.

Though the fort at the wall's terminus had been faithfully reconstructed, I could see from the fort's highest walls stretches nearby that were little more than crumbling mounds of packed earth in a parched landscape. I saw few other foreigners. There was little English-language signage to explain the construction and history of this portion of the wall. A Chinese dad who sported a T-shirt advertising a Charlottesville, Virginia, pizza shop gave me a little additional information:

"The fort is built mainly of rammed earth. Its initial construction occurred during the Ming Dynasty, starting in the 14th century. In addition to being a military fort, it was also a trading post along the Silk Road between China and the West," he told me.

When I asked how he'd come by his excellent English and his American-themed shirt, the man told me he was a cardiologist who'd done part of his training at the University of Virginia's Medical Center. Before I could ask many more questions, he politely bid me goodbye, rounded up his family, and departed the scene in an air-conditioned minivan that looked a great deal more comfortable than our taxi.

Still another decade passed before I visited an eastern terminus of the wall, in Hebei Province. This part of China was among the first to industrialize. Although rust belt relics existed in places, much of the area near the wall was prosperous and touristy. The beaches nearby are sometimes dubbed China's "Gold Coast." Beidaihe, the next town northward, contained beachside compounds used by senior Communist Party officials for summer retreats, away from the heat and smog of Beijing. There was a major expressway, with signage in both Chinese and English. Ice cream shops abounded, along with a liberal sprinkling of Western-style fast food restaurants: KFC, Pizza Hut, McDonald's. One restored wall section had a big commercial area alongside and was served by a public bus line; others were more remote and required a private car (now abundant among middle-class Chinese) or taxi. If the wall has a centuries-long history, many of its surroundings in Hebei were brand new.

In between Great Wall glimpses, I've had chances to view much of China both within and beyond the confines of the wall. I've been a tourist, a teacher, a guest, an explorer. All told, since that first visit in 1980, I've spent nearly three years of my life living or traveling in eighteen of China's twenty-three provinces, three of its five autonomous regions, three of its four independent municipalities, and one of its two special administrative zones. I've learned much from Chinese who've graciously disabused me of some of my mistaken notions about this big, ancient civilization and its modern development. I still have a lot to learn.

Many Chinese love folk and animal tales. A story my students would often retell for me involves a frog who lives at the bottom of a well. From the well, she can see a small disk of the sky above. One day, a turtle happens to hear the frog croaking as he passes by. He stops to chat. The frog invites the turtle to climb down to share space, but the opening is too small for his shell.

The turtle tries to describe some of what he has seen to the frog—wide expanses of sky stretching to far horizons, a sea so broad and deep that it maintains its level despite the most massive floods or droughts. He invites the frog to climb out to view the wider world. The frog instead decides to remain in the well, enjoying a more predictable life, viewing only the part of the sky she can see from the well's bottom.

At this point of my life, like the turtle, I've seen wide oceans. I've crossed the Pacific numerous times. However, like the frog, I can still see only small parts of a larger sky—my views have been shaped by my culture, my "American well," and the times through which I've lived. The sky I can see has been partially colored by my interest in civic engagement, my belief in peace, my concern for the natural environment, and my sense that all of us, sometimes in ways we cannot fully fathom, are interconnected.

This narrative is one older American woman's attempt to record reactions and experiences with China. What began with childhood stories and questions intensified during my young adulthood, as I came of age at the height of U.S. involvement in Vietnam's civil war, partially a "proxy war" in which China supported the opposing side. That war has left a lasting imprint on members of my generation, and continues to influence both governmental and interpersonal relations between Chinese and Americans. My subsequent travels in China helped transform a concern for my family's safety and a thirst for adventure into an enduring appreciation for China, its cultures, its peoples, and its magnificent scenery. I've found that the daily lives and aspirations of many Chinese are not totally different from my own.

A note about naming: I've changed names of most friends and acquaintances to preserve privacy. However, each anecdote describes a very real, unique individual. There are no composite characters here.

Chinese names are usually expressed either just with the family name, or with the family name first, followed by the person's given name. Often I've gotten to know people primarily by anglicized given names such as "Jane" or "Pearl" and have used these names in the text. For names of public and historical figures, I've used the alphabetic versions I'm most familiar with—Mao Tse-tung, Zhou Enlai, Chiang Kai-shek, Deng Xiaoping, Wen Jiabao, early Emperor Qin Shi Huang, and the poet Su Shi.

Digging Deeper

未入国，先问俗。

"There was a crazy fellow in town who undertook to dig through to China..."
Henry David Thoreau, *Walden,* 1854.

"Once upon a time, there were five Chinese brothers, and they all looked exactly alike. They lived with their mother in a little house not far from the sea..."
Claire Bishop, *The Five Chinese Brothers,* 1938.

My need to understand China got more urgent and more personal one spring evening in 1969. If I'd previously been intrigued by this big country on the other side of the world, I'd never considered that events and decisions there might impact me directly. I had just finished college and had started taking graduate education courses. I was about to get married. My future husband, Jim, had finally found a first job, difficult in 1969 for a recent male college graduate who was eligible for the military draft. Together we'd planned a small, simple wedding at the college chapel of Jim's former school in Virginia.

We were cobbling together furnishings from thrift shops and parents' attics for our first apartment, near the university campus in Baltimore where I was enrolled. On this Tuesday before Saturday's wedding, I arrived home nervous, but excited. Nearly everything on our respective to-do lists was checked off: Jim's former religion professor had completed our premarital counseling sessions and would perform the early afternoon ceremony; we'd obtained the needed marriage license; I'd sewn my bridal gown plus three bridesmaids' dresses, sending two ahead to bridesmaids who lived elsewhere; Jim had arranged for rented tuxes for the men, plus flowers and music. We were cash-strapped enough so that we didn't plan an extended honeymoon. We'd have a celebratory weekend, then get back to the apartment in time for work and classes the following Monday.

When I climbed the stairs and opened our apartment door that evening after class, Jim was already there. He looked dejected.

"Bad day at the office?" I cajoled, hoping to lighten his mood.

"No, not exactly," he grimaced. "Come sit with me and I'll tell you about it."

So far, our living room had only one comfortable chair. I sat on his lap.

"You know when you're expecting something bad to happen, and then it does, and you realize it's not quite as bad as you expected?" he asked.

"I'm not sure," I said, puzzled. "What happened?"

"Here, you read it," he handed me an official-looking paper.

It took me a minute to focus on the typed form that must have come in that day's mail. Jim was commanded by his draft board to report in three weeks for induction into the Army. Definitely a bad mail day. In early 1969, thousands of American young men were being conscripted each month to serve in the U.S. military. In those days before a birthday-related draft lottery, any male aged 19 to 26 not actively a student was unpredictably vulnerable. Jim apparently had drawn a short straw.

Briefly I went numb. Then, with a mixture of anger, fear, and acceptance that our priorities would have to be rearranged, I took some first stumbling mental steps toward a "plan B."

At least, I thought, we'd be able to have the wedding. I was prone to imagining worst-case scenarios. I worried that Jim might get sent to South Vietnam after basic training, since that's what had happened to his older brother, then serving south of Saigon at a base in the Mekong Delta. Both Jim and his brother might get killed. The best way I knew to get through my uncertainties and anxieties was to stay busy and to learn more about the background of the Vietnam War. Along with lots of other young people, I'd developed serious misgivings about the military draft and the war. Although I'd been writing occasional cheery letters to Jim's brother at his APO address, up until this evening, the war had seemed a little abstract. Not anymore.

As I tried to put Jim's news into context, I concluded that part of what I needed to do was to learn more about China. I'd read that Communist China was providing increasing levels of support to anti-government guerrillas in the south and to the North Vietnamese.

What, exactly, was China's role?

How did China's politics and people relate to the war?

What assumptions were driving the Chinese and American governments to spend more of their national budgets and manpower supporting opposing sides in the slaughter?

How could I figure out more about what was really going on in Southeast Asia and in China?

Luckily for us, Jim got a physical deferment and did not have to serve in the war. His brother came home relatively unscathed. Eventually the war ended. It would be another decade before I got a chance to see China in person, but my interest continued.

Gradually, I picked up more information about mainland China. Among the first things I learned were some basics:

In 1969, mainland China had a population of about 800 million, over four times that of the United States and over fifty times that of Taiwan, which at that point was recognized by the U.S. as the sole government of all of China. During the 1950s, "Red" China had been a close Communist ally of the Soviet Union, but it had since distanced itself from this "Communist big brother" with which it shared an extensive border.

The People's Republic of China (P.R.C.) is roughly the same size as the United States and occupies many of the same latitudes in the northern hemisphere. The country is shaped like a rooster, with its "eye" near the national capital, Beijing, and its feet in the South China Sea bordering what was then North Vietnam. Because the U.S. and the P.R.C. had no formal intergovernmental relations in the 1960s and early 1970s, it was hard to discern what was going on inside this opaque giant of Asia. I suspected that China would become an increasingly important actor on the world stage, one that I'd be smart to learn more about, regardless of what happened in Vietnam.

When I think back, I realize that I had been forming vague images of China and of Chinese life since early childhood. During my sandbox days, a friend had told me, "If you dig down far enough, you'll come out on the other side of the world, in China."

Following his advice, we'd tried several times to reach China. We eventually gave up—the ground beneath my homemade sandbox was too hard. What we mainly knew about China in our 1950s small Maryland town was that it was very far away. We guessed that the people who lived there were different from us. Our parents, usually when coaxing us to eat unpopular vegetables, told us that children there were starving. (Even at the age of six, I wondered how finishing my broccoli had anything to do with Chinese children.) Our family didn't know anybody who'd come from China. In fact, we knew few people different from our mostly working-class white families.

Early in elementary school, I read a children's picture book by American author Claire Bishop called *The Five Chinese Brothers*. The book, loosely based on a Chinese folk tale, tells the story of five nearly identical brothers with magical powers. One brother gets wrongly accused of murder, but the other four use their magical powers to prove his innocence. Since I had twin brothers who looked very much alike, I didn't think it strange for there to be five look-alike brothers. I enjoyed the book's illustrations of these young men with braids down their backs, though their braids were black as opposed to my reddish ones.

Some of the grown-ups around me worried about "Red" China. Nationalist forces on the mainland had been defeated in 1949 by Communist-led armies at the end of a lengthy Chinese civil war. The Kuomintang, as the nationalists were called, had retreated to Taiwan, but vowed to return to fight again. Between 1.2 and 2 million soldiers and civilians moved to Taiwan during the first few years following the end of the Chinese civil war. I remember anxious dinner table conversations about skirmishes and shelling along the ocean strait between the mainland and offshore islands. I recall my father poring over the book *Red Star Over China* as he sprawled on the living room sofa on Sunday afternoons. I later learned that this book was an account by Edgar Snow, the first Western journalist to interview Communist leader Mao Tsetung and to describe the Long March by Communist forces during the 1930s.

Until I was well into my teens in the late '50s and early '60s, my exposure to other places was mostly based on books I read, and later on documentaries and travelogues viewed on our family's black and white television. The demanding schedule of my father's small residential construction business precluded long trips. Then, the summer before I started high school, Dad closed down his business due to changes in the construction industry. He and Mom decided we'd go on a seven week, low budget, coast-to-coast summer car trip, visiting relatives along the way, catching parts of the Seattle World's Fair, and camping in national parks. While Dad mulled over what to do next as a job, we'd live frugally on Mom's school teacher salary. Partway through the trip, we stopped for a day in San Francisco. We walked around Chinatown and had dinner at a Chinese restaurant, where I munched lots of crispy noodles, ate chicken chow mein, and saw more red and gold dragon decorations in one place than I'd ever seen before.

My first Chinese-American friend was David Yang, who sat behind me in homeroom my junior year of high school. His parents had come to the U.S. from Taiwan and ran a small restaurant. We chatted fairly often about the courses we were taking. We even went to a folk concert together, but our relationship stayed casual and ended at high school graduation. During the same period, my mother, my grandmother, and I went to see the movie version of Rogers and Hammerstein's hit musical *Flower Drum Song* about Chinese immigrants in San Francisco. The movie's Chinatown seemed much more glamorous than the small glimpses I'd had on our cross-country trip.

After high school, I went away to college, mostly following a family tradition. Partly inspired by the example of a favorite high school teacher, partly in the interest of having a set of marketable skills, I decided to major in French and to get a teaching certificate. Like my mother, I could earn a decent living teaching school. I had vague plans to learn as much as I could about countries besides France, too. I attended a small Virginia liberal arts college then called Randolph-Macon Woman's College. I applied myself and got good grades.

Soon after I arrived at the Lynchburg campus, I learned through a library exhibit that our most famous alumna was Pearl S. Buck, a member of the class of 1914 who exerted a lingering influence at our school. Buck had come to America for college after spending most of her early life in China. As an adult, she'd returned to China as a missionary wife for over a decade. She wrote extensively about her adopted country. She won a Pulitzer Prize in 1932 for her most famous novel, *The Good Earth*. While at Randolph-Macon, I read this fictionalized account of the lives of non-famous, non-wealthy Chinese for the first time. In 1938, Buck received the Nobel Prize for literature.

Though Buck rarely visited the R-MWC campus, her name was widely invoked as an example of global citizenship. Much later, I learned that at her fiftieth college reunion in 1964, Buck was arm-twisted into giving a speech to that year's graduating class. Early in her generally uplifting talk, she noted somewhat pointedly that the European-American women who formed that year's graduates in fact represented a small minority of the global population.

"Less than a tenth of the people on this earth are 'white.' We have our place, but we are a minority group. If we do not know it, the other nine-tenths who are not white do," she reminded her listeners.

Buck was unable to return to China while the Chinese revolution and its aftermath played out from the 1940s onward. Still, until her long life ended in 1973, she remained optimistic about the potential for valuable East-West dialogue and collaboration. She adopted a number of children from China, helped found an adoption agency for multi-racial children, and advocated tirelessly for increased international understanding.

The more I learned about Buck, the more I felt that she was an excellent role model, one who'd been in many ways ahead of her time. However, in college, it never occurred to me that I'd one day visit or live in China. Even France seemed impossibly far away.

As my junior year approached, I decided against applying for a junior year abroad. Since my parents were providing most of the college funding for me and my younger sister and brothers, something so long-term, expensive, and far away would strain my family's finances. (Not inconsequentially, it would also provide a whole year when the boyfriend I was increasingly serious about could find another girlfriend.) Instead of crossing the Atlantic to France like several of my classmates, I found a summer job after my sophomore year in Montreal, Quebec, Canada—a self-funded, shorter-term venture for practicing French. For three months I sliced strawberries, ran the industrial-sized cream-whipping machine, and waited on customers at a Belgian waffle snack bar at Expo '67, Canada's first world's fair. I lived with my French-Canadian landlady. During my time off, I visited French-language sites and exhibits whenever I could. Sixty countries participated at Expo, including the Republic of China (Taiwan).

The China exposure I got at the fair came partly from the Taiwanese exhibit, and also from the Chinese-themed snack bar a few stalls away from where I worked. The Chinese-Canadian short-order cooks there made good, inexpensive fried rice. I also got some Chinese exposure through our snack bar's Chinese-Canadian owner. Near the end of the summer, Mr. Chan rewarded some of us who'd stayed longer than a few weeks:

"Please join me for dinner next Saturday," he told us. "We'll meet along La Gauchetiere Street near the intersection with Clark at 7 p.m. Then I'll take you to the best meal in Montreal."

Mr. Chan had reserved an upstairs banquet table for eight in Montreal's bustling Chinatown, which in 1967 spread for several blocks. The table was round, with a revolving Lazy Susan at its center—the kind you often find in Chinese ethnic restaurants worldwide. After skimming the menu, Mr. Chan put it aside and conversed with our waiter in rapid-fire Chinese. We ate superbly: spicy, succulent, crispy fish, seafood, meat, tofu, and vegetables, lots better than our neighboring snack bar's basic fried rice or the chow mein I'd sampled in San Francisco years earlier.

Once I returned to the U.S. at the end of the summer, I deferred further contacts with Chinese culture while I completed my college degree and got more deeply involved with the young man I would later marry. I didn't think much more about China until our marriage-eve draft scare.

My first full-time job coincided with my first year of marriage. I taught French in an urban junior high school. I was lousy at classroom discipline, letting the large classes of not-very-interested ninth graders get under my skin. Luckily for me, the information technology field was just opening up, with good job prospects for women. I became a computer programmer, communicating with "smart machines" in highly restricted, stylized languages not too different from the human languages I'd studied earlier. As our finances eased and the Vietnam era wound down, I had a first chance for real overseas travel. My language skills in French and German were still adequate enough to be of some use as we toured parts of Western Europe for seven weeks by bicycle and train.

While in the U.S., I deepened my readings on China and Chinese customs. For part of the 1970s, I had a subscription to an English-language magazine, *China Reconstructs*, published by an arm of the P.R.C. government. I skimmed it each month, looking at its pictures of rosy-cheeked peasants, imagining visits to this supposed workers' paradise.

Jim and I participated in one of the largest-scale Vietnam protests. We also joined an international short-term hosting and peace group called Servas, a small non-profit with chapters in over a hundred countries. Servas's primary goal was and is to foster global understanding. It seemed to me a positive step, a balance to the sometimes negative energy of war protests. Before "couch surfing" and Airbnb, or even the advent of the internet, Servas enabled international contacts through a curated printed directory system. It created a safe way for approved travelers and hosts from differing cultures to meet each other face-to-face for two-day home stays.

In Baltimore, I visited our local Chinatown. My favorite haunt was a second floor hole-in-the-wall restaurant called the "Mee Jun Lo." Situated up a flight of narrow stairs above a brass shop, the restaurant was open only in the evening after the downstairs shop had closed. Because Jim was working lots of overtime at a downtown Baltimore insurance company, our dinner scheduling was iffy. Often, we'd opt to eat at the Mee Jun Lo, not much more expensive than cooking at home. In those days, few people did carry-out. Customers filled up the restaurant's five or six mismatched, scratched wooden tables wherever there was an empty seat. Irene the waitress, a no-nonsense plumpish American with dyed black hair and a bullhorn voice, shouted orders to the cooks. Arabic numerals for the various dishes adorned both customers' English-language menus and the corresponding Chinese-character menu on the kitchen wall, making it possible for the Chinese family who ran the restaurant to get by with limited English.

"Nine, seventeen, sixteen, three, thirty-one," Irene would bellow above the din of conversation. My favorite dishes were sweet and sour pork and "moo goo gai pan," a chicken dish with mushrooms.

As I learned more about China's history and culture through my explorations and readings, the prospect that Americans would continue to be considered foes to the many millions of mainland Chinese bothered me. After all, China and the U.S. had been allies during World War II. Chinese immigrants had played important roles in U.S. history. The fiction that dictators in Taiwan, rather than dictators in Beijing, were the de facto rulers of all of China seemed more and more absurd.

In 1972 when U.S. President Richard Nixon actually went to China, I was thrilled. Nixon needed to extricate the U.S. from the costly, protracted quagmire that Vietnam had become. He also wanted to develop a counterweight to the U.S.S.R. He recognized that the Soviets and Chinese were not always on the best of terms. While in China, Nixon met with senior Chinese officials and signed the "Shanghai Communique," setting forth a "One China Policy" with regard to the mainland and Taiwan. Later, a second communique, signed by President Jimmy Carter on January 1, 1979, reestablished full diplomatic ties between the United States of America and the People's Republic of China after a nearly thirty-year gap.

In the mid-1970s, Jim and I temporarily abandoned overseas travel. By then, we'd completed several moves up and down the U.S. East Coast, first to Vermont, and then to Richmond, Virginia. In Richmond, we rented for a year then settled into an older two-story house in a mainly black neighborhood. Though I was a bit nervous at first, our neighbors were helpful and hospitable. Most were a generation older than we were with teenaged children. After another year or so, we produced two children of our own in rapid succession. Once they arrived, some of the neighborhood teens became our go-to babysitters.

We compensated for our need to stay closer to home by becoming more active as Servas hosts. We purchased a sleep sofa for visitors. Our first Richmond Servas guests arrived when our older son was still a baby. Both our children learned early that it was normal in our family to have overnight guests from other countries. As they learned to talk, they also learned to enunciate clearly and slowly for foreign visitors.

"What is your home country?" our older son would ask each new set of visitors at our first meal together. Often in the evenings, we'd get out the world atlas and compare the size and topography of our visitors' hometowns and regions with that of Virginia and the U.S. By the time our younger son was through kindergarten, he and his big brother had met Servas travelers from France, Germany, Denmark, Great Britain, Australia, New Zealand, Japan, and Israel. Servas, as it turned out, would soon provide my first opportunity to view parts of China in person.

2

First Sight

与君初相识，犹如故人归。

For more than 60 years, United States Servas has been bringing hosts and travelers together. A place to stay, friendship to begin, ideas to be exchanged, cultures to be shared, and world peace one conversation at a time: these are the reasons why you are invited to join us. U. S. Servas members are hosts and travelers of all ages, abilities and walks of life. Our more than 1500 hosts cover the whole spectrum of diversity. Through Servas' enlightening visits, participants come face to face with new peoples and cultures to further their understanding of the lives and concerns of others. Your participation and the friendships you'll discover can make a difference in your life and the world you live in.

U.S. Servas website, *www.usservas.org* 2017, accessed August 11, 2017.

One evening in late 1979, Jim and I had put the kids to bed and were unwinding after a long day. As I leafed through the latest Servas quarterly newsletter, I spotted an unusual ad.

"Wow!" I yelped, loud enough to draw Jim's attention away from the newspaper. "A group trip to China. Nearly three weeks for about three thousand dollars a person, including round trip air fare from the West Coast. Group trips aren't typical for Servas, but I'm sure this one would be interesting." Back then, traveling in China as an individual or as a family required special connections and permissions plus considerable added expense. Group travel made the most sense.

Over the course of the next few weeks, we garnered more details of the proposed trip then conferred with each other and with extended family. The previous year, after two years as a stay-at-home mom, I'd returned to the paid workforce, partly to retool my technical skills in a rapidly changing computer environment, partly to escape the isolation that often stalked young mothers during those "baby bust" years. Jim and I were feeling our way toward a realignment of our marriage partnership. Jim was somewhat less enthusiastic about the trip than I was.

"I don't think I want to go that far. Besides, it would be really expensive for both of us, plus babysitting would be an issue. Why don't you apply solo and see whether the trip actually happens or not?"

After considerable discussion, Jim agreed that if the trip actually took place, he would stay home with the children. My mother would visit and share childcare chores for part of the time I'd be away.

During trip preparations and the trip itself, I developed great respect for our American trip leader, Amelia Brown. Amelia was a long-time Servas member and a New York City native. Not long after she retired from her full-time job as a social worker in early 1979, she'd set to work to fulfill a long-deferred dream: to see mainland China before she died, minimizing her expenses and sharing the experience with others. Several years before her retirement, she'd established a part-time second career as a travel agent. Now, with more time to investigate, she checked out the few standard travel services that then provided China itineraries. She found their trips expensive, short, and with few opportunities for person-to-person contact. Not satisfied, Amelia established connections with others in New York and elsewhere who might provide better links to China. By the autumn of 1979, she'd roughed out a three-week schedule that would cover some of the tourist highlights, but also allow chances for more intercultural, interpersonal activities. Amelia thought twenty to thirty people would be about the right-sized group.

Itinerary established, Amelia sent out repeated notices of the upcoming tour opportunity to other peace-oriented travelers, while she continued negotiations with airlines and with China's national tourist service to get the best available rates and arrangements. She badgered friends and enlisted former colleagues to travel with her. She tapped into Servas through its newsletter and through NYC-area in-person gatherings.

After several months, she'd assembled an optimally sized group. Each of us got our passports updated, paid a deposit, and received any needed shots. In early July 1980 twenty of us gathered at the San Francisco airport, then took a crowded overnight flight across the Pacific. We lost a day crossing the International Date Line. Few of us managed much sleep on the jam-packed, noisy plane. As we made our final runway approach, I was alarmed at how close we skimmed to the water in Hong Kong harbor. I was greatly relieved when we landed safely at Kai-Tak International Airport at about 8 a.m. local time.

We'd next need to retrieve our luggage and complete customs formalities. After that, we'd regather to board the shuttle bus that would take us to our first Hong Kong hotel. A motley crew, we were a mixture of blacks and whites, ranging in age from eleven to seventy-three, from both U.S. coasts and places in between. Over half of us were women travelers, adventuring alone or with friends.

Once through customs, we slouched in the entry lounge, jet-lagged, confused, and culture-shocked. We waited for Amelia to find our shuttle. Overcoming any jet lag of her own, Amelia got us safely settled into our first hotel with enough time for naps before our next scheduled activity. More than once during our three-week trip, Amelia would use her social-worker mantra on Americans and Chinese alike:

"Start with the client where he or she is."

I was one of the younger adults at age thirty-three. There were a few family groups, the largest led by a retired airline pilot who joined us in Hong Kong, along with his wife and two college-aged children. My roommate was Maria Dixon, a middle-aged African-American woman from East Harlem whom I first got to talk with at the Kai-Tak arrival lounge. Maria and our trip leader Amelia made up part of a core group of eight travelers from greater New York City. If I'd sometimes found Vermonters upon first meeting them rather laconic and slow to speak, or Virginians overly genteel, I thought at first that these New Yorkers were rather brash, loud and prone to complaining.

However, these traits in Maria benefited me almost immediately. We had been shown to our room. We'd hefted our suitcases onto our respective luggage racks. I opened my smaller bag, preparing to unpack.

"Hold it! Don't unpack yet." Maria commanded. "It stinks in here. This won't do. And we're right next to the elevators. We'll never get any sleep for the noise. I'm going to get us a better room."

I'd been hesitant to say anything about a chemical smell, probably a recent paint job. Now that Maria mentioned the noise, I realized that the frequent "dings" we'd been hearing would become more bothersome overnight. Before I could respond, Maria went down to the hotel desk to complain. A few minutes later, one of the elevator dings announced her return, accompanied by a staff member who apologized in halting English, gathered our luggage, then reinstalled us in a less fragrant, quieter part of the hotel.

Over the course of the trip, I learned that Maria had tackled the difficulties of getting to China with determination and ingenuity. She'd borrowed money from friends to help cover trip fees and incidentals. She'd packed carefully but stylishly. She'd gotten background materials about the cities on our itinerary from travel agencies and the library. If occasionally complaining about poor service was a part of Maria's makeup, it was one I could live with.

Hong Kong in 1980 was bustling, crowded, and very vertical. We got guided tours of several standard landmarks. Most days our itinerary was jammed from early morning until evening. The height of our tour was an aerial tram ride up Victoria Peak, a nearly 2,000-foot mountain over-looking Hong Kong's coastline and the islands beyond. Along the slopes of the peak, wealthy estates shared space with ramshackle shantytowns.

At the end of our first full day of sightseeing, Maria and I found an inexpensive restaurant not far from our hotel. It had a picture menu. We pointed. We shared a good meal of chicken with cashews and a stir-fried vegetable dish. Other patrons rubbernecked—we were the only non-Chinese there. Once we'd finished eating, I was able after several tries to find out where the restrooms were.

Either at this restaurant, or someplace else less touristy on the 1980 trip, I got my first exposure to Chinese squat toilets. Over time, I came to realize that average Chinese were more likely to use squat than sit toilets. Immediately, I realized that my muscles were not accustomed to squat-ting; they were especially unaccustomed to getting up unassisted from a squatting position. In subsequent travels and stays in China, I got ex-posed to a wide variety of squat facilities. Except in the most impover-ished rural areas, squat toilets came with individual stalls. In most apartments, schools, restaurants, and shopping areas, toilet stalls had tile floors, with the toilet area raised about eight to twelve inches above the base of the floor. In the middle of the raised area was a saucer-sized hole. Within easy reach to one side was a toilet paper holder. Under-neath it was a receptacle for gently used toilet paper, so less refuse went down the toilet hole, avoiding potential clogs. More and more facilities had flush buttons. Where there was not a mechanized flush, an atten-dant made regular rounds to ensure that facilities stayed clean. On trains, squat toilets were metal, with foot pads to either side of a bowl-shaped receptacle that also flushed. Recently, most squat facilities on trains have added a grab bar, making it easier to get back up. I've learned to practice squats as part of an exercise regime, but no matter how much

I try to stay flexible, this aspect of regular Chinese life is one I've never truly mastered.

Amply fed, adequately toileted, Maria and I made our way safely back to the hotel. The following morning, we were up and about before the day's official tours. We wandered into the nearest park, where some locals played ball or did slow, graceful exercises. Once back in our room, we turned on the television, looking for a weather report.

"Whoa, look at those costumes!" Maria exclaimed as we caught bits of a Chinese melodrama with lots of elaborate headdresses and frequently staged sword fights.

A channel switch brought us a cartoon.

"Popeye sure sounds strange in Chinese," I giggled.

We never did find a weather report, and it probably wouldn't have helped, anyway. The weather was steamy and changeable. One early morning I ventured out before the day's planned activities and got caught in a sudden downpour. My umbrella helped, but was unable to shield me entirely. I stopped under the eaves of a large building, nearly alone along a major street that was not yet as frenetic as it would be later in the day. At the other side of the street, a largish rodent scampered to get out of the rain. I was grateful it was headed away from me.

Another day, I skipped the optional group tour and took a local train northward to Sha Tin, located in the New Territories between Hong Kong municipality and the border to the People's Republic. Sha Tin was famous for its horse racing track. It wasn't racing season, so the empty track was just a distraction from my goal—a Buddhist shrine I'd read about in a local guidebook.

As I tried to find the path to the shrine, a local young man spoke to me in English.

"May I help you, lady?" he asked, flashing a big smile.

I took out my guidebook and pointed to the description of the shrine. "Do you know where this is?" I inquired.

"No problem," he said. "Follow me."

He led me down a couple of side streets and partway up a path marked with symbols for the shrine, then demanded a substantial tip. Thus reminded of the occasional ulterior motives of young men with big smiles, I produced a middling tip, bid him goodbye, and huffed my way solo the rest of the way up a dirt and gravel track. Before long, I arrived only slightly out of breath at a hillside shrine nestled in a relatively open grove of trees.

In front of the shrine were several small sand-filled urns on pedestals where earlier visitors had placed sticks of incense. Their smoke mingled with the smells of tree leaves and damp earth. The shrine's central feature was a glass-topped sarcophagus containing the embalmed body of a local Buddhist guru. I could not understand the all-Chinese signage, so I was limited to the description I'd read in the guidebook—the guru had lived to a ripe old age, requesting that his preserved body be left on display for pilgrims. Physically tired from the hike, I also felt satisfaction that I'd found a small snippet of less touristy Hong Kong. I trudged back down the hill and caught the next train back to the city center.

On our fifth morning in Hong Kong, we awoke early, gathered our luggage, bused to the long-distance train station, and boarded a through train toward the People's Republic and the gateway city of Guangzhou. Everyone was excited. We would finally enter formerly forbidden territory.

"I wonder if they'll frisk us," said our youngest member.

The train took a while to leave the station. I worried about the border crossing. I had flashbacks to an earlier incident when I'd gotten stopped at the Canadian border because I lacked a work visa. Back then I had to spend the night on a bus station bench and it had taken an intervention by my Canadian boss the next day before I was allowed to continue. There everyone had spoken English, but here next to no one did. Would I manage to make it through? How would I cope if I didn't?

Finally I relaxed a little and began to take in more of my surroundings. Our train car was plushly furnished. Maria shared one set of seats with me. Other group members filled up most of the single train car into which we'd been segregated. Our comfortably upholstered seats had white lace doilies on the arm rests. Mounted high above the center aisle was a loudspeaker and a small television set, and at one end of the car was a restroom with a sit toilet.

The windows to our train car had been newly washed. Even while we sat in the station, there was plenty to watch: wiry Chinese men scurried by with loads balanced on long shoulder poles. Crates and boxes, some with labels in English as well as Chinese, sat piled on handcarts or laid out in batches along the platform. Meanwhile, a mixture of men, women and children shoved toward the doorways to other cars of the train. Many of these passengers had bundles wrapped up in worn-looking cloths, knotted at the top. Some women carried babies in slings on their backs. I would witness this shoving phenomenon many times over in China throughout the years. I wondered what was causing this sense of urgency—past famines or times of lack?

As the train began to move, an official-sounding voice barked something over the loudspeaker. Later, patriotic music blared. At one point, the television screen lit up with a short black and white feature. Our Hong Kong-based Chinese tour guide, Shirley, who would stay with us for our entire journey, made no comment. The rest of us had no clue about the words, but the body language and costumes made the message abundantly clear: smugglers and spies would be promptly, severely punished. As our train approached the border crossing, I held my breath. When it slowed, but did not even stop, I let out a long sigh.

The sky, overcast when we'd left Hong Kong, grew darker. Before long, rain was lashing at our windows. We could still see the relatively flat countryside, crisscrossed here and there by windbreaks of tall, narrow trees on pathways raised a few feet above the surrounding fields and paddies. Peasants with flimsy plastic raincoats, wearing sandals or barefoot, moved quickly down the paths beside the windbreaks. Some had on the conical palm frond hats I'd earlier seen on American television specials about the exotic East. In a couple of fields, farmers who seemed unaware of the bad weather plodded along behind water buffalo, their attached ploughs making ripples in the muddy paddies. The landscape mirrored the television program we'd just watched—colors muted, motions blunted, a drab counterpoint to the lights, colorful outfits, and unrestricted movements within the cheery bubble of our foreign tourist train car.

Once deposited at our air-conditioned, high-rise hotel in Guangzhou, we did the minimum of unpacking for this single night stay. That evening, we ate our first Chinese-style group banquet while we gazed out the floor-to-ceiling windows of our banquet room at the now-intermittent showers. After dinner, we boarded a tour bus for a gymnastics exhibit a few miles from town in what looked like a converted high school gym. The thousand or so bleacher-style seats were almost completely filled with foreign tourists like us.

My neighbor to one side of the bleachers was not a member of our group.

"Where are you from?" I asked.

"I grew up near London, England," he responded in a crisp British accent. "I'm stationed in Hong Kong with the Hong Kong Shanghai Bank. I've brought my family to Guangzhou for the day to sightsee and catch an acrobatics performance. Aren't they marvelous?"

I agreed. During intermission, we all went outdoors. Under a clearing sky, our hosts treated us to slices of incredibly sweet local watermelon, then led us to a communal spigot and wash basin where we got most of the stickiness off our hands. We watched another hour or so of human contortions, leaps, and balancing acts that hardly seemed possible, then were whisked by tour bus through dimly lit streets back to our hotel. The following morning we boarded a plane for Beijing.

Our Beijing area itinerary contained the customary tourist venues: the Forbidden City, the Great Wall, the Ming Tombs, the Summer Palace. I found that July could be just as sultry and rainless in Beijing as it was in Richmond. The sun glared down through a slightly hazy blue sky. In Beijing, as in subsequent cities where we spent more than a day, we were assigned a local guide in addition to Shirley. Our Beijing guide, Mr. Zhang, was probably in his early thirties and quite proficient in English. He also was more open to answering questions, even about somewhat sensitive topics, than I'd expected.

Our Beijing lodgings consisted of the ground floor of a vacant foreign students' dormitory in a university district northwest of the city's center. The dorm rooms had electric fans, but were still somewhat stuffy. One evening after supper, I went out for a cooling walk with Claudia, a group member about my age. As we returned from a leisurely circuit of the neighborhood, a young Chinese man approached us. He seemed to be in his mid-twenties.

"Hello," he said in English. "How do you enjoy our city?"

"We like it very much," said Claudia, "but the weather is hot."

"Where are you from?" he asked.

"We are from America," I replied. "We've come on a group tour to several Chinese cities. It's our first time to visit China."

Then I asked a question of my own. "May I ask, are you a student, and if so, what are you studying?"

"I learn computer science," he said, "and I also study English. I do not get many chances to practice with foreigners." We continued for a while, chatting back and forth in "tourist English." Claudia and I each gave him a postcard from our respective hometowns. He seemed ready to talk longer when a guard at the entrance to our dorm snapped at him in Chinese. Our acquaintance looked apologetic, murmured a quick "Goodbye," and was gone.

On our second full day in Beijing, our guides took us to a small Buddhist shrine and monastery in a less-frequented area of the city. The shrine, recently reopened, had been badly damaged during the Cultural Revolution, a nationwide convulsion that raged from 1966 to 1976. Mao Tse-tung had launched this attempt to revive post-war China's revolutionary spirit. As it evolved and sometimes skittered out of control, the Cultural Revolution stressed the need to destroy traditional beliefs, often interpreted to include the landmarks that reinforced them. Mr. Zhang was eager to be among the first tour guides to visit the newly accessible shrine. We met a middle-aged monk and asked about his life. Mr. Zhang provided this simplified English version:

"For over ten years I have been a monk. I am happy to return to this small monastery. The past several years I worked in the countryside. While we monks were away, our Buddha shrine was damaged. We repair it while we resume our Beijing lives as monks. I live simply. I like to work in this place."

In the vicinity of the shrine, we noticed cracks in the walls of some of the older brick buildings. When asked, Mr. Zhang responded that they had most likely been caused by the Tangshan earthquake, a natural disaster that rocked parts of northeastern China in July 1976.

Our four days in Beijing were followed by another plane flight, this time to the western Chinese city of Xi'an. In the countryside nearby, we saw early excavations of the "terra cotta army," an array of life-sized individually crafted statues of warriors, horses and chariots commissioned by early Chinese emperor Qin Shi Huang to guard his burial tomb. The first of the statues had been discovered accidentally in 1974 by peasants digging a well.

Our accommodations in an older-style guest house in the Xi'an area were my favorite of the trip. Our group totally filled the seventeen rooms in that low-slung facility at the end of a narrow valley with a steep hillside rising behind it. The room that Maria and I shared had for me the ultimate luxury: a sunken bathtub with hot and cold running mineral water, quite an extravagance in arid western China.

One evening when we returned by tour bus from the day's sightseeing, we found that an overhead spotlight had been set up in the front courtyard of our guesthouse. A large local crowd had gathered to view the flowering of a night-blooming cereus, a species of cactus that blooms only at night, and only once each year. The cactus was anchored in a large clay pot. Its vine had been trained up a bamboo trellis, with its flower bud about ten feet in the air. We joined the crowd, watching the large milky white flower unfurl, breathing in its sweet fragrance.

Our overall visit went by in a whirlwind, with stays in Hong Kong bookending about two weeks in the P.R.C. In addition to Guangzhou, Beijing, and Xi'an, we also traveled to the central Chinese province of Henan, visiting its capital city, Zhengzhou, and some of the surrounding countryside.

One afternoon we stopped near the small city of Luoyang to see the Longmen Grottoes Buddha carvings—a set of both large and small Buddha images graven into a rock face along one shore of a local river, stretching for nearly half a mile. Some of the images had been damaged during the Cultural Revolution, but enough were intact or restored to be quite impressive.

After gazing at the largest Buddha, I spent some time scrambling along hillside paths to view some of the smaller niches. Once, I got stuck with unstable rocks on all sides of me. A young Chinese man nearby reached out his hand to steady me. I was surprised, relieved, embarrassed, all at the same time.

"*Ni hao*," I ventured. "*Xie xie.*" (Hello, thank you.)

After I reached firmer ground, we took pictures of each other with our respective cameras. Using hand gestures, I got my rescuer to follow me to our Hong Kong-based tour guide further down the slope. Shirley helped me learn that my temporary hiking companion was a cement worker from Zhengzhou who'd come sightseeing while in Luoyang for a conference.

Most of our travels through rural Henan were by air-conditioned minibus. It was harvest time. Our drivers would sometimes swerve to avoid damaging the ripened grain spread on sunny pavement to dry. At a few rest stops, our group could interact briefly with local people. Even our guides had trouble understanding their thick local accents. We were just as much a tourist attraction to the locals as they were to us; once in a while we all shared shy smiles.

The final leg of our P.R.C. journey consisted of a 28-hour train ride south from the central rail junction city of Zhengzhou through the Chinese countryside back to Guangzhou. Our rail car, the very last one on the train, was usually kept locked. For meals, we were let out and escorted to a dining car near the middle of the train. Our trajectory took us through a baggage car that included caged live chickens and ducks among other parcels, trunks and boxes. We also traversed several sleeper cars geared toward less affluent Chinese travelers—the foam mattresses, lace curtains, and Western-style restrooms in our "soft sleeper" tourist car seemed even more luxurious contrasted with the flimsy mattresses and more crowded bunks for non-VIP travelers.

Guangzhou, which had seemed underdeveloped when we first arrived there from Hong Kong, now seemed wealthy. It was far better off than many of the rural areas we'd seen by bus in Henan or from the train windows on our return trip. A guide explained that many Guangzhou residents had relatives in Hong Kong who sent them appliances and other consumer goods. After another overnight stay at a Guangzhou hotel, we crossed back into Hong Kong.

The main activities of our final two days were shopping and eating—Hong Kong's restaurants offered more varied fare than the ample but rather predictable group banquets we'd been served during our P.R.C. stay. I tracked down a bilingual Chinese friend of a friend who treated Maria and me to "dim sum."

Herbert showed us to a table in a large penthouse dining room with floor-to-ceiling windows overlooking Hong Kong and some of its harbors. Waitresses and waiters appeared through swinging kitchen doors, parading among the tables pushing carts loaded with lots of small plates and little bamboo steamer baskets. The concept is somewhat similar to the tapas meals that have recently gained popularity in the U.S. However, in dim sum, all the choices are already cooked and on display.

"Excuse me, what are those?" Maria asked as a waitress pushed past us, her cart laden with several plates of mysterious-looking vegetables.

Herbert translated:

"Those are lotus root," he pointed at one offering, "and these are bok choy steamed with garlic."

"I'll try the bok choy." Maria chewed a couple of mouthfuls, then gave a thumbs-up sign.

Another cart approached.

"And those?" I asked, pointing to some pale gelatinous items shaped like peace symbols.

"Those are chicken feet. And those," he pointed at some small, doughy white spheres, "are steamed buns filled with bean paste."

Before we finished, we'd sampled a dozen different dishes from several carts. I never did figure out how to chew the chicken feet, but the steamed buns were delicious. After our meal, Herbert led us to a side street with some small shops—quite different from the huge mainland "Friendship Stores" where foreign tour groups were routinely deposited and strongly encouraged to buy expensive art and craft items. I found some children's picture books plus a few remaining small gifts for family back in the U.S.

Once I returned home, I developed the pictures I'd taken. Anyone who would listen got an earful about my marvelous trip. I began to explore ways to get back to China in a year or two for a longer stay. Ideally, a subsequent visit would include a work component and would allow Jim and the children to come, too.

In late 1981, an American friend who worked with "ACTION," then the umbrella U.S. governmental volunteer agency, phoned to describe an exciting new prospect: a chance to teach computer skills in China using English as the language of instruction. Volunteers would be recruited in the U.S. through the Peace Corps. Although that agency limited direct assignments to single adults, this program in China would be administered through the United Nations, so spouses and minor children could also come.

By that time, Jim and I had each logged nearly a decade of varied computer software experience. The children were just starting elementary school—old enough to require less supervision, at ages when they could benefit immensely from exposure to Chinese spoken language, which children pick up much more quickly than adults. It seemed like a perfect fit. We completed an initial round of paperwork, submitted our applications, and crossed our fingers that we would be among the initial volunteers chosen.

3

A Door Closes, A Window Opens

失之东隅，收之桑榆。

"It's hard to uproot yourself and really become yourself in another soil, but it's also an opportunity, another kind of growth."
Chinese-American author Ha Jin, interviewed in *Paris Review,* 2009.

During the 1980s our chances for a joint Peace Corps assignment in China fell victim to "tennis diplomacy." In contrast with the early 1970s, when the initial thaw in U.S./P.R.C. governmental relations was heralded by "ping pong diplomacy," the early 1980s brought a temporary chill. In August 1982, Chinese rising tennis star Hu Na, touring the U.S. with a Chinese-sponsored team, left her teammates and sought refuge with friends in California. She later filed a request for political asylum, claiming she would face persecution if she returned to China. Once the U.S. State Department granted her request, the still-fragile diplomatic ties that had been building between the U.S. and the P.R.C. snagged.

It would take another ten years before the U.S. Peace Corps began operations in China. During subsequent travels in China, we've met several active Peace Corps volunteers, but our personal paths have diverged from any sort of American government-related program.

Though a China Peace Corps assignment did not pan out, we got several nibbles about other overseas assignments. One snowy weekend morning in February, our home phone rang.

"*Allo,*" a French-accented voice said. "*Madame Batterson, s'il vous plait?*"

Switching gears, I found an appropriate French response. Our conversation continued in a mixture of languages. The caller was a United Nations staff member in Paris who wanted to know if Jim and I might be available for U.N.-related assignments in French-speaking Africa. The international line occasionally became garbled with static, but I could hear and understand most of what he said.

"We'd like the two of you to go to Burundi to help with economic development."

"Burundi?" I repeated. "Where is that, exactly?" I hoped that my lack of geographical knowledge would not scotch our chances right off the bat.

"It's a small, underdeveloped country in central Africa."

(Glancing out at our frigid landscape, I wondered if Burundi would be warm year-round.)

I responded, "We'll need to know more about the assignments before we decide."

The caller said he'd send us more details by postal mail. To me, a former French major who'd had nearly ten years of teaching and business background, the assignments sounded as if they could be a sort of long-deferred "junior year abroad," and one I'd get paid to take.

The following week, I checked out the only book I could find about Burundi at our city's public library. It turns out that the country is a New Jersey-sized nation that had briefly been a German, then a Belgian colony before independence in the early 1960s. Situated across Lake Tanganyika from the huge mid-African conglomerate then called Zaire, Burundi had received little development support from colonial powers. Its post-independence trajectory included periodic political assassinations, uprisings and ethnic conflicts. It had a general lack of physical or financial infrastructure, a tropical climate with accompanying tropical diseases. Sounded risky.

Over the next few weeks, we got additional information from the U.N. postal packet and from a former volunteer whose assignment the previous year had been similar to the one I was being asked to fill. I would live in a U.N. compound in the country's capital city, Bujumbura, teaching computer and accounting skills in French at a central government office. My project would support a nationwide network of consumer and coffee-producing cooperatives. Not quite so risky, after all. Unfortunately, there was not a correspondingly suitable assignment for Jim who spoke little French. To further complicate matters, while we were trying to reach a decision, Jim got a tantalizing Richmond-based job offer from one of his computer consulting clients.

It took nearly half a year of soul-searching, family discussions, and sleepless nights before Jim and I agreed to split the family, we hoped only temporarily. In Bujumbura, Burundi, I would pursue my dream of international development assistance integrating many of the language and computer skills I'd acquired so far. In Richmond, Virginia, Jim would pursue a parallel dream of improving software quality. Jim would keep our older son, who at that point had serious asthma, in the U.S. with him. Our younger son, about to enter first grade, would come to Africa with me. Our adventures during my stay in Burundi may one day become a different travel memoir, but for this story, the China connection is what remains important.

The connection took a few months to develop. In early 1984, the same American friend who'd earlier steered us toward the Peace Corps again phoned my husband:

"I know Jinny's going to be away for a while and that you have a spare bedroom," she began. "You've long been interested in China. How would you like to host two Chinese goodwill ambassadors who are coming to Richmond next month to learn more about American culture?"

Without skipping a beat, Jim responded, "I'm game. Can they cook?"

It would be our family's first experiment in long-term hosting. Previous experiences hosting shorter-term international visitors through Servas and other friendship organizations provided some helpful guidelines. In addition, these first Chinese visitors, Mr. Wang and Mr. Chen, were very eager to make a good impression. I may never know what they thought of America. I don't think they've ever returned for a lengthy visit. I'm sure there were a few tense times while they stayed with Jim, but most reports I got via letters and phone calls were positive.

Wang and Chen quickly adapted to the household routines. After a few samples of Jim's culinary talents, they took over the majority of the cooking. They taught our son the Chinese expression he most wanted to master: "*Kan dianshi*"—"let's watch television." They stayed for a semester, attending classes and seminars at a large public university near downtown Richmond, while getting a thorough exposure to an American household in a mid-sized American city. Jim took them grocery shopping, introduced them to American high school basketball, took them on sightseeing excursions to nearby Charlottesville and Williamsburg. He even showed them his tax forms and explained the process of filling out a 1040 as he completed it in April. In turn, Jim and Justin attended events where Wang and Chen described or demonstrated Chinese culture.

Two young Chinese adults added an interesting twist to the ethnic mix of our multi-racial Richmond neighborhood. Occasionally, a short-term Servas guest would also be added for a two-night stay. Jim wrote me about one particular weekday dinner including a Servas guest from Ireland. Supper that evening also included Shawn, an African-American neighbor about Justin's age who came for dinner and homework help a couple of times a week. Mary O'Neill, a twenty-something Servas traveler, was just finishing up her Richmond stay, her first with an American family. Her shy demeanor and freckled fair skin made her seem like an Irish country girl straight out of the movies.

Wang had set the table in the dining room, with chopsticks beside each plate. Justin and Shawn came downstairs as Jim served up the spaghetti sauce and noodles in large bowls, family style. Mary soon appeared from the guest room that had been cleared for her visit. Our son did a quick scan of the table settings and the serving dishes, then made a brief detour to the kitchen to get forks and spoons for the non-Chinese.

Over dinner, the conversation ranged widely: third grade math, high school basketball, Richmond museums and landmarks, how to eat spaghetti with chopsticks, and the lingering influence in China of the "Gang of Four" (leaders of a radical political faction that had included Mao Tse-Tung's actress wife, discredited after Mao's death in 1976). Shortly after dinner, as the rest of the family cleared off the dishes, Mary excused herself, saying she needed to go upstairs to write a letter to her mother.

"I wouldn't dream of snooping in someone else's mail," Jim wrote me, "but I sure would like to have known Mary's impressions of our multi-cultural family."

Several months after Wang and Chen returned to China, Jim hosted Dr. Hu, a physician from the northern Chinese region of Inner Mongolia. Like Wang and Chen before him, Hu got a glimpse of some middle-class Americans living their daily lives. He helped with the house-keeping in this all-male household, cooking an occasional meal and tidying up. Hu's previous experiences with carpet sweepers required a little adjusting—the notion of an electric appliance to clean rugs was foreign, as Jim found out one day when he discovered Hu carefully sweeping the carpet with the electric vacuum unplugged.

By the time Stuart and I rejoined our Richmond household in late summer 1985, our family's hosting pattern with Chinese visitors had become somewhat established. It took us a few months to get re-accustomed to life as a four-person family in the U.S., and to find enough paying work to keep from dipping further into our savings. Meanwhile, the influx of Chinese students and scholars to the United States was really taking off. We found that we could rearrange furniture and sleeping assignments slightly so that there was still a spare room, and that we could budget so that having an "extra" who paid minimal rent would be workable. Deng, a postgraduate student of microbiology, moved in with us in January 1986. Our reunited family later welcomed several successive graduate and post-graduate students from China.

Deng's arrival came in the midst of a cold winter. He had grown up in the northeastern part of China, so the cold didn't bother him—winter had been an enduring part of his reality. However, he at first had difficulty adapting to American dietary habits. His funds were limited, and he wanted to take a packed lunch to work with him each day. I packed him a lunch of a sandwich and fruit similar to what I prepared for the children. I doubt that cheese or baloney sandwiches had been part of his Chinese reality, but he didn't complain. I was able over time to adapt our evening meals to include more Chinese-style dishes.

While Deng lived with us, he sometimes used our micro-computer to help in his research. Although our Apple II-e was far from cutting edge in the U.S., Deng told us that it still exceeded the computing power he'd had available at his lab in China before coming to America. His stay was not all work, however. We went on weekend excursions to area attractions, following the precedent set with Wang and Chen. One outing that did not work out quite as planned was a summer inner tube float on a relatively calm portion of the nearby James River. It had not occurred to us that Deng would need sunscreen. After several hours in the summer sun, he had a bad burn that took several days to subside.

In mid-1987, Deng got a grant to do further research work in a different city. Before he left, he recruited his replacement: Lin, a fellow student he knew by reputation. Lin arrived during the summer and worked at one of the medical labs downtown until the fall semester started. On evenings when he was not too tired, he tutored me in entry-level Chinese, marking the first of my many intermittent attempts to improve my Mandarin ability beyond the most basic tourist phrases. After the dinner dishes were cleared, we'd sit at the dining room table going over lessons, using a book Lin had found with several hundred words and phrases. I'd stammer them out, looking at the phonetic pronunciation, desperately trying to mimic the correct intonation for each syllable in tonally sensitive Mandarin.

Regardless of how badly I butchered the intonation or pronunciation, Lin reassured me:

"*Hao, hao!*" ("Good, good," pronounced roughly like "how, how.")

Before summer's end, Lin lived through an inner-city resident's nightmare with us: an overnight home break-in as we all slept. The thieves took most of our somewhat outdated stereo and computer equipment. They also made off with the used bicycle Lin had purchased to save money on commuting. Once we'd finished with police and insurance reports the following morning, we apologized to Lin. We said we'd buy him a replacement bicycle and would understand if he chose to move out and find other lodgings. He stayed on. We became a bit more security-conscious.

Angel was our first woman housemate. She arrived around Christmas time and joined Lin at our house. She immediately charmed our younger son, who established a habit of sitting beside her on the sofa as our family watched evening news together after dinner.

"May I brush your hair?" he'd sometimes ask.

"That would be nice," she'd typically respond, and turn sideways in front of him so he could run a soft brush through her long black hair. Angel was every bit as pretty as the picture of her that Lin had put on his dresser shortly after he'd arrived.

Because of holiday travels, it took a while before I noticed that Lin had been relegated to an air mattress on the floor of the former baby nursery at night, while Angel slept alone in the double bed in Lin's guest room. I'd heard that customs for unmarried couples were stricter in China, but was baffled by this sleeping arrangement. It was not until after they had married the following June (temporarily breaking our younger son's heart) that Angel explained how little she and Lin knew of each other until she arrived in Richmond. They'd only met briefly in China as Lin was about to board a plane for his study in America. Angel was the airline ticket agent who handled his flight.

By the time Tang, our final graduate student visitor, came to live with us, the community of Chinese students and scholars in Richmond had expanded to the point that most students began rooming together, rather than boarding with American hosts. In early 1989, Tang moved out to share an inexpensive apartment near the medical college. The community of mainland Chinese expatriates from many different regions of China formed closer bonds in the alien culture of urban America. I missed the daily Chinese exposure, but was relieved, too. I had less time and energy to share with long-term guests. As our children entered their teens, their activities and demands on our time and attention increased.

At some point during this period, Jim and I joined the Richmond, Virginia, chapter of United States China People's Friendship Association, USCPFA for short. USCPFA is a small non-profit whose mission is to improve intercultural understanding and promote friendships among ordinary citizens in America and in China, sometimes more easily said than done. During its early days, many chapters of the USCPFA were politically radical, but the group had diversified over the years—the Richmond chapter was likely one of the more sedate. Joining the group seemed a logical progression from our hosting activities and a way to gain a wider window on China and all things Chinese. I enjoyed attending their occasional banquets and movie showings at the Chinese Embassy in Washington, D.C., often around the time of the Chinese national holiday on the first of October.

Our USCPFA chapter hosted an annual June weekend swim party, picnic, and overnight stay for Chinese embassy officials who were mostly younger staff members, part of a rotating group who came to Richmond in succeeding years. They relished a chance to experience life "outside the Beltway" and to engage in something other than embassy routine. For several years we were a weekend host family, enjoying an additional low-key chance to expand our understanding of a rapidly changing China.

On a Saturday evening we'd gather in the shaded backyard of an older USCPFA member. Her small swimming pool was inviting in the often hot, humid weather.

"This is what is called a 'potluck' dinner in American English," our hostess would explain. Each Richmond family had brought a dish—some Chinese-style, others Western-style, nearly always including at least one take-out bucket of KFC fried chicken and one spicy whole fish. After cooling swims for the children and a bountiful outdoor supper, the party would split up. Each host family would take one or two Chinese embassy staffers home.

In accord with China's continuing policy of "reform and opening," more and more of the embassy personnel posted to the United States came as couples. Some embassy wives (ranking officials were still nearly always male) attended Richmond swim weekends with their husbands. I remember lively Saturday evening conversations in our living room. We could broach some, if not all, hot-button issues such as the implications of the one-child policy and the status of cross-straits cooperation with Taiwan.

My recollections are of well-informed, curious, polite representatives of the P.R.C., deeply committed to their country's continuing progress, if not to all the vagaries of changing policies in China and in America.

4

An Inconvenient Spotlight

灯不拨不亮，理不辩不明。

"If only it were all so simple! If only there were evil people somewhere insidiously committing evil deeds, and it were necessary only to separate them from the rest of us and destroy them. But the line dividing good and evil cuts through the heart of every human being. And who is willing to destroy a piece of his own heart?"
Alexandr Solzhenitsyn, *The Gulag Archipelago, 1973.*

"It's a strange thing, but reporting on horrors can actually leave you feeling more optimistic about our species. The truth is that side by side with the worst kind of evil, you tend to find the greatest altruism and nobility."
Nicholas Kristof, who reported from Beijing during spring, 1989, interviewed by *The New York Times* at the 25th anniversary of the Tiananmen crackdown, June 4, 2014.

Around June 4 each year, I frequently see a short video clip captured by an American journalist; it's the somewhat blurry image of an unarmed Chinese civilian approaching a line of military tanks on Chang An Avenue in central Beijing on June 5, 1989. The footage has become iconic for many Western China-watchers. The man emerged from a large crowd. He wore a white shirt and dark trousers. He carried a small sack in each hand, as if in the midst of a shopping trip. He stood in front of the lead tank, which pivoted to move around him. The man maneuvered to stay in front as the tank swerved several times. Finally, the tank stopped. The man climbed up and tapped on the turret. For a minute or two, he conversed with the driver, presumably asking him to alter course and turn back. Then "tank man" climbed back down and soon was swallowed up in the crowds lining the avenue. Few are sure what happened to tank man after that. Before long, the tanks began rolling again.

By the time student-led demonstrations erupted in Beijing in late April 1989 our family had provided long-term housing for seven mainland Chinese students and scholars. We'd also hosted several sets of short-term visitors. I had friends in the Chinese-American and Chinese expatriate communities, some from mainland China, others from Taiwan, and still others from Hong Kong. I'd read lengthy works about Chinese history by American China scholars. On a regular basis, I skimmed some of the English-language publications of the P.R.C. government, discounting much as propaganda, but enjoying the pictures of life in different parts of China. I was forming a slightly less blurred picture of China and its relations with other nations.

Over the years since my first China visit in 1980, I'd been exposed to some of the complexities of relations between and among mainland

41

Chinese, Taiwanese-Chinese, Chinese-Americans, and Americans of other backgrounds. Our mainland Chinese visitors would tell us sketchy stories of their lives and families back home. I was sure some details got left out or sanitized. I learned that many mainland Chinese resented the "century of humiliation" between 1840 and 1949, when large portions of Chinese territory and trade were dominated by external, almost colonial powers. Taiwanese-American friends whose parents or grandparents had retreated across the Taiwan Strait in 1949 or shortly afterwards remained distrustful of P.R.C. Chinese. Similar fault lines existed between mainlanders and residents of the British colony of Hong Kong.

My older Honolulu-based cousin typified the attitude of many Americans. The most recent time I visited him, I asked if he'd ever been to China.

"No," he told me. "At one point in the early 1980s, I had an offer to teach auto mechanics there. It would have been a very profitable gig financially. I thought about it. But then I remembered night duty when I was in the U.S. Army in the early 1960s, stationed near the demilitarized zone separating the two Koreas. It was scary. The notion that there were millions of Chinese soldiers willing to back up the North Koreans stayed with me. I decided I really couldn't trust the Chinese. I didn't go."

The more I learned about Sino-American relations, the more aware I became of harmful attitudes and incidents from our mutual pasts. American attitudes toward China and Chinese have often been condescending, racist, hostile, sometimes openly violent, and vice versa. Chinese first came to the U.S. in large numbers after gold was discovered in California in 1848. During that period, China was beset by both foreign and domestic armed conflicts. Two Opium Wars, the first spanning 1839-1842, the latter 1856-1860, were won by European powers who demanded territorial concessions and expanded trade powers. An intense internal conflict, the Taiping Rebellion of 1850-1864, killed tens of millions of people. Thousands of young Chinese men, most from the coastal provinces of Fujian and Guangdong, boarded boats across the Pacific to escape China's turmoil and participate in the gold rush. Although few Chinese immigrants got rich, many stayed on and later played an important role in the construction of America's transcontinental railroads. Then, during U.S. economic downturns in the 1870s and 1880s, backlash against Chinese immigrant labor grew sharply. In 1882, the U.S. Congress passed the "Chinese Exclusion Act," a law specifically banning Chinese immigration to the United States. The law was sporadically enforced until it was finally rescinded in 1943.

During the late 19th century in China, anti-foreign sentiment grew, especially against some of the practices of foreign missionaries. This discontent erupted during 1899-1901 in what came to be called the Boxer Rebellion. Over a thousand U.S. Marines participated in the international force that eventually suppressed the rebellion and relieved foreign legations in Beijing. Some Americans were among the missionaries and soldiers killed. In 1911, China's final Qing dynasty fell, ushering in a brief Chinese republic. That government soon gave way to a set of regional warlords with little loyalty to anyone but themselves. A small Communist party group was established in Shanghai during the 1920s. Its military wing, aided by advisers from Russia, began fighting against other factions. In the early 1930s, Japan took over northeastern China, establishing a puppet state, "Manchukuo." Several years later, the Japanese military launched a full-scale invasion, which ended only with Japan's global defeat and surrender in 1945. After that, a civil war between Communist forces and Kuomintang (or Nationalist) forces resumed. Hostilities ended with the victory of Mao Tse-tung's forces on the Chinese mainland in October 1949 with remnants of the Kuomintang retreating to the island of Taiwan. Soon afterward, the U.S. government chose to recognize the Taiwan-based Republic of China as the sole legitimate government of all China. It would be nearly thirty years before full diplomatic relations between the People's Republic and the United States of America were re-established.

As 1989 began, I mulled over the many peaks and valleys in U.S.-China relations weighing the sense that intergovernmental relations between our two countries, after a full decade of direct diplomatic contact, might have achieved a more stable footing. Contacts and programs to promote cultural, scientific, and educational exchanges between U.S. and Chinese citizens were proliferating. I crossed my fingers that, along with official ties, more friendships between average Chinese and average Americans might actually become possible.

The global power structure was changing. Soviet President Mikhail Gorbachev was revising many policies of the Union of Soviet Socialist Republics (U.S.S.R.) and embracing more openness, *glasnost*. In China, the economy had taken off after leader Deng Xiaoping in late 1978 began steering a course away from a centrally controlled economy toward a more market-oriented one. Still, results were uneven and complaints about government corruption increased. Dissidents in China called for government reform. Public protests popped up, often mirroring struggles between hard-liners and reformers within the Chinese Communist Party. Once one party faction gained the upper hand, protests were squelched and dissent again disappeared underground.

Then, in late April 1989 several thousand students from universities in Beijing began demonstrating on central Tiananmen Square, mourning the April 15 death of a deposed former reformist official. At first, the demonstrations attracted little notice. As time passed, the protests escalated. They began to include increasing demands for government reforms and with that larger and larger numbers of area workers and local citizens joined the protests. Even some members of the People's Liberation Army (China's military) joined in. One Western journalist's estimate put the peak number of demonstrators on the square at over one million. Protests also broke out in other large cities and provincial capitals.

In early May, hundreds of members of the international press corps arrived in Beijing to cover the upcoming state visit by Soviet President Gorbachev, the first meeting between Soviet and Chinese heads of state since Nikita Khrushchev's visit in 1959. I wasn't a big television watcher, but I'd sometimes catch short clips about the protests as I wandered past the TV evening news on my way somewhere else. On May 19, as Gorbachev returned to Moscow, the Chinese government declared martial law in Beijing. Undaunted, the protesters continued, with about a thousand students participating in a hunger strike that had begun on May 13. The escalating stand-off made me nervous.

On Monday, May 29, an American couple active in USCPFA's

Richmond chapter invited chapter members and several local Chinese students to an informal evening gathering at their house. I went and listened. The students had been paying close attention to unfolding events.

"Protests correct," one student proclaimed. "Too many times success based on bribery, on payoffs, on family connections. Should have more safeguards for average Chinese, not just high officials' children."

On my short drive home, I imagined my best possible resolution to the protests: some of the demonstrators' demands would be met; the protests, which had recently shown signs of losing momentum, would gradually subside peacefully; senior Chinese government officials would put a positive spin on their roles in moving the country forward. I was proud of the students, if worried that some were overplaying their hand.

That Friday, I left work early and drove up the interstate highway to Maryland to visit my parents and my extended family. It was a journey I both relished and dreaded—my first chance in several months to reunite with other family members. My father was in failing health, suffering from diabetes and memory loss. Mom kept my out-of-town brother and me posted by phone, but it wasn't the same as being there. Dad sometimes got confused and belligerent, especially at night. Mom was having trouble getting enough sleep. My in-town sister and brother had stepped up their involvement in Dad's care to help Mom out, but we were inching toward considering putting Dad in a nursing home. I badly wanted to share time with Mom, Dad, and my sister and brothers before Dad's memory deteriorated even further.

By the time I arrived, both my brothers and my sister, along with their spouses, had already gathered at my parents' roomy house. I parked and came in the kitchen door.

"Hi," I beamed at my out-of-town sister-in-law as we hugged around her slightly expanding belly. "How's the next arrival coming?"

"The little one is fine," she answered, "but it continues to make me queasy, even in my fourth month."

"I've been drinking lots of herbal teas," my sister put in, rubbing her own expanding tummy. "They seem to help."

Once I'd stowed my overnight bag in a guest bedroom upstairs, I came down to the living room, where Mom introduced me to the young

Chinese couple who were lodging with her and Dad for the semester. He was a doctoral student at a nearby university. His wife was largely pregnant, expecting their first child in a month or so. Three pregnant women all in the same house was a bit unusual.

"Your sister-in-law will have a son," the Chinese father-to-be told me. "Only boys make their mothers so sick."

After a light supper around an extended dining room table, we swapped stories of previous pregnancies across several generations and two continents. My in-town siblings left with their families. The rest of us bedded down early. Dad had a quiet night.

Saturday morning, we chatted idly and toured my parents' yard—the towering tulip poplar tree at one side of the house, the various smaller trees and shrubs Mom and Dad had planted to screen off the back part of the yard and reduce lawn maintenance as they grew older. The home place was still very beautiful. Some of the apple trees held onto a few late blooms while the azaleas had just finished theirs. By midday, our extended family had reassembled. We had a quick lunch together, then gathered in the living room, put our chairs into a large circle, and played "yarn ball," a game Mom had improvised to help include Dad in the weekend's activities.

Dad's reflexes were still good, so he nearly always caught the ball and threw it on to one of us. Though his ability to converse was compromised, throwing the ball back and forth connected him with the rest of us in a different way.

The radio was on in the next room, mostly providing background noise. Because of the time difference, Beijing's overnight hours of June 3rd and 4th corresponded to Saturday afternoon, June 3, in Maryland. We almost missed the first bulletin of the military crackdown in Beijing. We turned on the television news. We kept it on. We were stunned. The younger generation, including my parents' Chinese houseguests, sat up late into the evening discussing what had just happened.

What we mostly saw and heard were violence, chaos and darkness: sirens wailing, shots or explosions sounding, some people running in panic, others improvising bandages and stretchers for the wounded. Even reporters on the scene in Beijing had difficulty grasping the scope of the crackdown and the extent of resulting deaths. Estimates by some Western journalists ranged as high as 10,000, with an initial figure of around 2,600 from the Chinese Red Cross. Early on Sunday, June 4, Maryland time, my parents' resident Chinese scholar went to Washington, D.C., to join other protesters at the Chinese embassy there.

Our family weekend sputtered to a halt. On Sunday afternoon, I returned to Richmond and began trying to contact former Chinese housemates who might still be in the United States. As it turned out, Deng, Lin, Angel, and Tang were all still in this country and safe for the moment. All were anxious about their futures and very concerned about friends and family members back in China. Other Chinese cities had seen crackdowns of varying degrees of brutality and loss of life. I was relieved for our former lodgers, yet achingly sad at the tragic end to the protests. In the following days and weeks, I sometimes almost wished for memory loss like Dad's—it would have been easier to stay oblivious to what was going on.

In mid-June, 1989, our USCPFA chapter met to decide on a response to Tiananmen and its aftermath up to that point. We wanted to register our dismay with Chinese Embassy officials in D.C., some of whom we'd come to know personally. During several hours of painful discussion, everyone had a chance to vent and to provide input.

"I always knew in my heart that the Communist government could not be trusted," insisted an older American member who had spent much of her childhood with a merchant father in Tianjin, a former treaty port in China's northeast.

"If we react too harshly, it's only likely to increase distrust and repression," cautioned another American who'd spent a year teaching in Xi'an several years before.

In the end, we crafted a carefully worded note decrying any loss of life and recommending restraint in dealing with surviving protesters. We also agreed to halt embassy visits and swim party weekends indefinitely.

Tiananmen's aftermath quickly impacted official relations between the Chinese and U.S. governments. U.S. President George H.W. Bush immediately stopped arms shipments and canceled high-level talks about nuclear cooperation with China. In late June, the U.S. Congress passed more sweeping trade restrictions and economic sanctions. The next spring, President Bush issued an executive order permitting Chinese students who'd been in this country during and just after the protests to remain here indefinitely. Its scope was later expanded by Congress.

Whenever I've traveled to China since, I've been cautioned to avoid bringing up the events of spring 1989. I comply. I've seen no mention of the 1989 protests in official P.R.C. media. I've heard that security at Tiananmen Square is especially tight around the June 4 anniversary. The one at-length Tiananmen discussion I've had with someone from China occurred around our American kitchen table in mid-autumn, 1994. By then, our house's bedrooms were filled with a mixture of biological and intentional family—my husband and me; our younger son, about to finish high school; a high school exchange student from France, Philippe; and an international exchange teacher from southern China, Mr. Huang, our first Chinese long-term visitor since the crackdown who also became a dear friend.

Huang was in his mid-thirties, with a wife and teenaged son at home in China. This was his first trip to a Western country. About two months into his year-long stay with us, he struggled with his teaching assignment of promoting Chinese culture and language at a nearby inner city elementary school, quite different from the elite high school where he'd previously taught English in China. He missed his wife and son. He still had difficulty understanding American idioms and accents.

The evening's exchange was prompted by an American TV news clip about the Congressional debate over U.S. renewal of "most favored nation" trading status with China. U.S. media coverage of this then-annual debate nearly always included archived footage of events in Beijing in June 1989. Huang paid careful attention to the footage and the TV commentary as did the rest of our temporary international family. Once the news broadcast was over and we'd finished a somewhat tense

supper together, our French visitor broached the subject of the Tiananmen protests and their resolution.

"It's a shame that so many of the surviving protesters had to flee to
Hong Kong or overseas," he remarked. "They could have helped a lot
with economic development if they'd been allowed to stay and con-
tribute without being threatened or jailed."

Huang at first said nothing.

"From what we saw on television, there must have been many casualties," our son said.

"What did you hear about the protests, Huang?" I wondered, hoping to at least partially defuse the teenagers' impassioned rhetoric.

"Not many people died," Huang informed us. "Most of those killed
were soldiers trying to put down a counterrevolutionary mob."

"But most of the demonstrators were students or ordinary citizens,"
our son retorted. "And we saw people who weren't soldiers lying bleed-
ing on the streets. We saw ambulances and stretchers. We heard gun-
fire."

"How can you tell what happened?" demanded Huang. "You were
thousands of miles away. I was at home in China. What I saw and read
in the newspapers confirmed that the soldiers were the main casualties.
I'm glad not more of them were killed."

"Your newspapers tell you only what they want you to hear,"
Philippe put in. "We saw the tanks and tracer bullets on television in
France. How can we doubt what we saw with our own eyes? Were you
in Beijing?"

"I've never been in Beijing," Huang admitted, "but my father served
in the People's Liberation Army (China's military) during the 1950s.
He was a brave soldier. He fought hard for our country. Our military
would never harm another Chinese, not unless they were trying to destroy the revolution. Our military serves the people—they were only
doing their duty in Beijing in 1989 to restrain counterrevolutionaries
who wanted to bring down the government."

After a few more exchanges, we realized that we would never con-
vince each other. The media spins on the protests and crackdowns by
our respective communications outlets were selective and diametrically
opposed. About all we could agree on was that good governance requires

considerable self-restraint on the part of both governments and their citizens. Our media exposure was hugely different. Our backgrounds were, too.

As I got to know Huang better, I pieced together some of the traumas and periods of turmoil that he and his family had already experienced. Huang's earliest years corresponded with a severe drought and a disastrous early attempt to collectivize Chinese agriculture (1959-1962). Food was scarce. His mother had sometimes gone without in order to feed Huang and his younger sister. Over a decade later, near the end of the Cultural Revolution, Huang had been forced to interrupt his studies to spend three years doing manual labor in the Chinese countryside.

Now, he was a senior teacher with a steady income and a chance for international travel. Maintaining social stability was a high priority. He believed, and wanted to believe, official reports about the counterrevolutionaries who'd tried to disrupt Chinese progress and order by demonstrating at Tiananmen Square.

I try not to dwell too much on Tiananmen or what it might represent. As an American whose ancestors fought on both sides of the American Civil War, I know that my home country is not immune to civil strife. That epic struggle caused over 600,000 military deaths and immense civilian suffering. A century and a half after its end, we still find it painful to have an open, honest discussion of the impact of chattel slavery in the United States of America. We have trouble, too, confronting the persistence of various forms of racism, classism, sexism, and demagoguery.

5

Joint Custody of a Dream

同心筑梦，携手圆梦。

What happens to a dream deferred?
Does it dry up
Like a raisin in the sun?
Or fester like a sore—
And then run? —

        from "Harlem," by Langston Hughes, *Collected Poems,* 1951.

During the summer of 1995, our family constellation changed a lot. First Huang, then Philippe, and then our younger son Stuart all left—our international visitors to their home countries, Stuart to a university about four hours' drive away. For the first time in nearly twenty years, Jim and I were alone in our house. We were unsure how to adapt.

We'd succeeded financially beyond our expectations. We seemed to have raised caring children well on their way to adulthood, yet we'd suffered losses, too: first my dad, then Jim's father had died during the previous few years. The summer of 1994 Jim had surprised me with a fabulous trip through parts of Turkey and of newly-freed Eastern European countries for our twenty-fifth anniversary. We'd relearned how much we enjoyed traveling and experiencing exotic places, but doubted we'd be able to afford anything quite so lavish again soon, with two sets of college tuition bills looming. What would we do to fill our now-less-hectic time?

Not long afterward, the phone rang. Our caller introduced herself as the director of the Japan-Virginia Society, a small non-profit that worked to encourage both business and cultural links between Virginia and Japan. She'd gotten our names and contact information from a mutual friend who volunteered placing international high school students in American homes.

"I hear that you are experienced international hosts with some spare room in your house," she began. "We're looking for low-cost long-term accommodations for a business intern who'll be arriving from Japan next month to help with administration and outreach from our downtown Richmond office."

You can guess what happened next. We came to call the succession of interns our "Japanese daughters." Our first-to-arrive daughter, Akemi, told us that Japanese business culture was not friendly to women. Even outstanding women college graduates were frequently relegated to being "tea ladies," office workers assigned to run errands and serve tea to the male "salarymen" whose gender automatically guaranteed their superior status. Akemi did not want to remain a tea lady. In her late twenties, she came to the U.S. to intern for a year, hoping that international experience and improved English would widen her subsequent career options. I admired her spunk. Over time, I also came to cherish the consideration and reserve that were part of her culture. As Akemi completed her year with us, she overlapped for about a month with her successor, Mamiko, who also began living at our house. We were sad when Akemi left, but Mamiko brought her own joys, including an American suitor, Rob, who'd met her while on a work assignment in Japan.

Rob became a frequent visitor that autumn. I enjoyed watching their romance unfold, but was relieved not to be a biological parent to either of them as they sorted through the challenges of a deepening intercultural relationship. Observing their young love, I was less and less sure of an appropriate role for the next phase of my own life.

Our days of intensive parenting were over. I'd reached a plateau professionally. Jim and I had created a small software consulting business and had enough steady clients to keep us busy. We'd moved to a larger house with a huge yard and garden. We'd reached a peak of earnings, but also a peak of expenses, with house payments and college tuitions for two increasingly independent, but not yet self-supporting young men. Every once in a while, I craved some excitement beyond the routine of work, family, visitors, gardening, and short-range trips.

The excitement I got wasn't what I thought I'd wished for: a small, painful breast lump erupted around Halloween. It didn't go away like my other menopausal symptoms. Jim, not usually a nag, this time insisted I get it checked out.

"I know your most recent mammogram was normal, but a lump like this may not be. Get a referral and find someone who can tell you what's going on."

Biopsies are no more fun than mammograms I soon found out. The first one seemed inconclusive, so I was scheduled for a follow-up just before Thanksgiving with a more invasive procedure that had to be performed at a hospital. I arrived at the hospital early, only to find that I was not on the surgery schedule. After I'd tried for half an hour to determine why not, I got a phone call from the surgeon.

"I thought you'd been notified," he began, "your previous pathology report showed some highly malignant cells. There's no need for a surgical biopsy."

It turned out there had been a series of communication problems. I'd been out of town for a week, and though the doctor's office had tried repeatedly to reach me, they'd been unable to get through. "Sorry, you have cancer," is not an appropriate message to leave on someone's answering machine. The surgeon apologized for the abrupt way I'd learned of my diagnosis, then made time in his morning schedule for a brief consult with Jim and me. At first I was so busy bristling with anger at the way I'd been told that I didn't grasp the seriousness of the news. Afterwards, trying to digest alternatives of mastectomy, lumpectomy, radiation, and/or chemotherapy, Jim and I dragged ourselves home. In the chaos, I'd forgotten to alert Mamiko to my changed status. She met me at our front door, smiling broadly:

"So glad all your tests are done," she told me, not noticing my dejection at first. "I brought you a small gift—gourmet coffee to help pep you up."

Even as we all reeled from the bad news, Jim and Mamiko gave me much-needed hugs and encouragement. After a while, the two of them left for their respective offices. I stayed in the house, unusually alone. I was still shaky, but grateful for time to grieve and to begin to come to grips with this latest challenge.

I went upstairs. I sank into my favorite chair in my favorite room, a small, south-facing "reading room" off the master bedroom. Sunlight filtered into its bay window through the last leaves on the mulberry tree in our front driveway. It shone on a bookcase Dad had made for me when I was in high school. As I pressed slowly back and forth in the oak rocking chair he'd also hand crafted, I wondered how much longer

I might have to enjoy the gently slanting sunshine of late autumns. I confided my worries to my journal, which seemed to help.

A few days later, after I'd calmed down some and decided on initial surgery, I asked Mamiko if she'd prefer to find a different host family.

"It's not likely to be all that cheerful around here for a bit," I cautioned. "You and Rob deserve a place that's not quite so stressful."

Mamiko stayed. She managed her own complex life with grace and aplomb, at the same time brightening mine and Jim's with gentle humor, supportive cards and cheery email messages. It took nearly a year before my surgery and follow-up treatments were over. The doctors I consulted all recommended a regimen of six to nine months of chemotherapy to kill off any wandering malignant cells that might cause a recurrence. Some evenings, when I was too tired from treatments to fix dinner and didn't want to risk a digestive upset from Jim's limited culinary repertoire, Mamiko intervened.

"Let me cook. I really enjoy it. I can prepare some Japanese dishes that my mom used to make for me when I wasn't feeling well. There's a special soup with ginger that should be easy to digest."

During my treatments, I was lucky to have clients who let me work part-time on a flexible schedule. As I started to regain strength, I realized I neither wanted nor needed to return to work full-time. I had the luxury of rearranging the balance of work, family, service, leisure and travel in my life. I'd never previously gotten around to compiling a "bucket list." That was for after retirement. Now faced with the possibility that I might not live until normal retirement age, I began to plot another international trip, this time to Asia.

By the time Japanese daughter number five, Momoyo, came to live with us, we'd made our final college tuition payment. I'd healed enough physically and psychologically for an extended overseas jaunt. Momoyo acculturated quickly. She let us know she'd be happy to housesit if we traveled to Japan. Her parents, plus the families of our four earlier "daughters," were eager to meet us. They would try to cram payback for our yearlong hosting of their daughters into our short visits and their hospitality would reduce our travel expenses to a fraction of standard costs in normally expensive Japan.

Although our trip at first focused on Japan, China beckoned. Ever since my first China trip in 1980, I'd wanted to share with Jim some of the sights and culture I'd been exposed to then. Besides, we reasoned, China was nearly next door to Japan. It seemed a shame to get so close and not visit. We could spare the extra time from work. We'd built up our savings again. We had a varied, flexible, reliable client base. Now that the children were grown and on their own, we had fewer family responsibilities. Because our expenses in Japan would be low, we'd be able to afford a China add-on. Hotels and travel in China would be cheaper.

We knew that China had changed a lot since my first visit twenty years before. I exchanged letters with Huang, now back at home near the southern city of Guilin, a couple of times a year. An older American friend, Joan, part of our U.S. China People's Friendship chapter, had developed deep China connections by teaching English there for several semesters during the 1990s. For eight months a year, she lived in Richmond's sister city of Zhengzhou, the capital of central Henan Province. We read her letters of various adventures and misadventures with interest. Whenever she came back to the U.S. for holidays, we listened to her stories in person, pestering her with questions.

Official U.S./China governmental relations had continued to zigzag. The furor over Tiananmen had gradually died down. Expanding trade between the two countries brought different tensions: the U.S. expressed mounting concerns about intellectual property rights and software piracy. During the late 1990s, China objected strenuously to NATO responses to the civil war in the Balkans. Still, even during tense times, there were few clamp-downs on international visitors to China. U.S. Peace Corps volunteers continued to work in several Chinese provinces.

From the U.S., we were able to arrange our international flights, along with hotels and "city capsule tours" for Shanghai and Beijing. We learned that individual foreign travel in China was a lot easier to arrange and much less restricted than in 1980. So, as the first year of the twenty-first century turned to spring, Jim and I embarked on a joint visit to China.

If you had asked me, before this 2000 trip, what my favorite part would be, I'd have told you it would be showing my husband a few of the fabulous sights I'd seen solo a generation earlier. That was part of my dream. In addition, it turned out that the encounters that mattered most to both of us, that fed our subsequent dreams, were not in our original itinerary.

I began to notice changes as soon as we arrived at Kansai International Airport near Osaka, Japan for our flight to Shanghai, China. We arrived in plenty of time, checked in, and found our boarding gate. In a roomy departure lounge, we waited with the other passengers most of whom were Asian. We guessed that passengers going to Shanghai would likely be Chinese, much more affluent Chinese than those I'd met in 1980. Back then, no private citizen would have been able to afford plane travel. Besides, few would have been allowed to leave the country.

Now nearly everyone seemed at ease, almost blasé. Most were in Western-style dress: business suits for the men and elegant dresses for the women. Nary a drab blue Mao jacket. No roughly tied cloth bundles bulging with goods and snacks for a long trip. Women wore make-up. Their luggage was name-brand and stylish. A few children traveling with their families amused themselves with video games on hand-held game consoles.

As the time to announce the flight neared, our Japanese ground crew sprang into action. They placed several conspicuous signs in the boarding area. Printed instructions, in Japanese, Korean, Chinese, and English, were consistent with the highly regimented, highly efficient Japanese style we'd noticed earlier in subways and train stations. According to the signs, the plane would be boarded by groups from back to front, minimizing confusion in airplane aisles and streamlining the boarding process. Each passenger had an assigned seat and boarding group on the nearly full flight.

The smartly uniformed, carefully coiffed young Japanese woman in charge of boarding announcements looked around nervously and took a deep breath.

Before she could say "*Ohayo gozaimasu*" (Good morning, ladies and gentlemen), most of the other passengers had mobbed the departure gate. Never mind their smart attire and stylish luggage—they pushed and shoved and elbowed each other to be near the head of the line. This bottleneck at entrances was one I'd already seen in China and would see reenacted with regularity during subsequent trips. Was this what famines did to people, I wondered?

Once we landed in Shanghai, Mr. Li, a long-term government employee representing the China International Travel Service, met us at the airport arrivals area. He held aloft a sign: "Mr. Batterson."

"Welcome to China," he greeted us in British-accented English. "I will be your Shanghai guide. Please let me know whenever there's anything I can do to make your stay more pleasant."

With that, he shepherded us and our luggage into a waiting taxi and escorted us to our hotel. We spent three nights and parts of four days in Shanghai, which impressed us as dazzling, yet somehow less "Chinese" than I expected. The spotless windows lining one side of our 28th floor room in a 30-floor French-run hotel overlooked busy Nanjing Road. Pedestrians, shoppers, and window shoppers streamed by on the broad sidewalks. Behind a few of the mid-rises on the opposite side of the street, I could just make out the outlines of some lower, less well-kept buildings. I never got to see them up close.

Our second day, Saturday, April 15, was a day with no pre-arranged tour. Out for a walk, I noticed a small temporary stage set up in the pocket park next to our hotel. It was decorated with lots of red balloons, streamers, and large character banners. About midday, a young people's band assembled on the stage and began playing patriotic music. At roughly the same time, a big-screen TV nearby started broadcasting a continuous loop of a short talk by a serious-looking Chinese woman in an official-looking suit. Beneath the televised speech was a crawl in Chinese characters that I couldn't understand. Young women in seductive outfits trolled the audience, giving out free samples of a new health drink. It took me a while to find someone bilingual enough to understand my English questions and then to explain to me what I'd just witnessed: an annual effort to get Chinese to pay their taxes on time.

April 15 seems to be a day that citizens on both sides of the Pacific are not too scrupulous about observing.

After Shanghai, we spent the next five days of our customized journey in the area of Beijing, where we saw together some of the same sites I'd visited in 1980. Many tourist venues we traipsed through were just as picturesque and exotic as before, albeit spruced up and somewhat more crowded. However, my favorite Beijing encounter occurred on a rare clear, windy day when we'd gone on our own to sightsee near Tiananmen Square. As we approached, we saw several box kites bobbing and weaving above the horizon.

Once on the square itself, we found several older men preparing their heirloom dragon kites for flight. The kites, nearly fifty feet long, had extensive tails made of circles of paper glued to lightweight wooden rings, all linked together by three parallel strings that ran the kites' entire length and could be used for steering. The rings were decorated with sturdy feathers for stability. Only when the tail was almost fully aloft was the dragon-shaped head of the kite attached and quickly pulled skyward. Watching the kites dip and swirl above the square helped heal some of my memories of Tiananmen's recent history.

After Beijing, we'd be venturing into parts of China where foreign tourists were less plentiful. Mr. Li had helped us get needed airline and hotel reservations for our next two cities: Zhengzhou, in the central province of Henan, and Guilin, further south in the Guangxi Zhuang Autonomous Region. The Zhengzhou visit would be a partial repeat for me, but would include a new connection courtesy of our American friend Joan.

While we were planning our itinerary, Joan, a decade or so older than us, had suggested that we include the city of Zhengzhou. Her arguments were persuasive—she had enjoyed several years of post-retirement adventure as a foreign English teacher at a magnet high school there. She'd maintained contact with several Chinese former colleagues and arranged to have them give us a personalized area tour. Jim and I were toying with the idea of becoming foreign English teachers outside the U.S. now that we were empty-nesters. With Joan's help, we could scope out some prospects.

We boarded a morning flight from Beijing to Zhengzhou, just missing the onset of a spring dust storm, a brownish haze that approached from the northwest as our plane gained altitude. At the Zhengzhou airport, well away from the storm, Joan's teaching colleagues welcomed us with bouquets. They supplied a car and driver to take us to our hotel, arranged an evening banquet on the Thursday we arrived, then a full day of sightseeing on Friday. We'd be on our own for the weekend, but would visit their school the following Monday.

We spent most of Saturday wandering in a large park not far from our hotel, listening to groups practicing traditional Chinese music, joining in briefly in a couple of English-language songs they were familiar with such as "Do-Re-Mi" and "Edelweiss" from *The Sound of Music*. On Sunday, we'd arranged through the hotel staff to have a car and driver for an all-day excursion to the Shaolin Temple, a historic site recently reestablished as a burgeoning center of Chinese martial arts. Part of our route took us through a major coal mining region. The paved road was about two lanes wide, without lane markers. As we crested the top of one rise, several vehicles abreast, we met heavily loaded coal trucks, also several abreast. Horns blared; brakes screeched. Somehow, everyone adjusted paths so no collisions occurred.

Much of the Shaolin complex had been recently reconstructed or refurbished, though the dioramas of various martial arts poses displayed in an open courtyard were somewhat dusty. Later, we wandered through a large walled area at one side of the complex.

Approaching a rare other foreigner, I inquired, "What are those tall pillars?"

"They are steles honoring former abbots of this monastery, going back over a thousand years," he let me know.

Before we left, we saw boys and young men moving single file downhill through the complex. Each carried a plastic bowl and small towel. On our return trip, the heavy traffic we met was mostly composed of luxury vehicles driven aggressively. We later learned that these BMWs and Mercedes belonged to the newly wealthy parents of the young men enrolled in martial arts training at the temple. We were glad to have seen Shaolin, and even gladder to be deposited safely back at our Zhengzhou hotel.

Our Monday school visit got off to a slightly late start due to rush hour traffic. The headmistress gave us a brief introduction to her school, then led us to a classroom to observe a sample lesson by a Chinese teacher of English. Accustomed to what I remembered of American high school classrooms—lots of discussion and interaction with teachers—I initially found the more formal style of this lesson taxing. As the teacher droned on in a mixture of Chinese and English about some obscure point of grammar or translation, I had difficulty staying awake. Students sat quietly listening behind crowded rows of twinned wooden desks piled high with books and notebooks. I couldn't tell if any of them understood what was being said.

At midday, we went off-campus for a lengthy restaurant banquet arranged by the head of the foreign languages department. Several dishes were new to me, including one composed of buds from a local tree. Another was a sort of fruit soup in a watermelon "broth" that managed to be sweet without being cloying. Sharing a meal seemed to loosen the atmosphere.

Near the end of the school day, after refreshing naps in the teachers' lounge, we were escorted to a conference room. We sat in plush chairs and got introduced to the remaining Chinese teachers of English, plus about a dozen of the top English students. The students' first several questions were predictable:

"Do you like China?"

"What is your family like?"

"What kind of apartment do you live in?"

"Do you have a Chinese name?"

"What do you think of Zhengzhou?"

"What do you think of our school?"

We tried to be clear, concise, and measured in our answers, alternating responses and doing our best not to interrupt each other. Gradually, the questions grew more complex:

"What is the main difference between schools in China and schools in America?"

One young man was adamant, instructing us and questioning at the same time:

"Zhengzhou is not a tourist city; it is a workers' city. Why have you decided to come to Zhengzhou?"

Too soon, it was time to return to our hotel.

After Zhengzhou, we'd scheduled a week's stay in the city of Guilin, in southern China, before our trip's final few days in Hong Kong. Guilin appealed to us for several reasons:

- It anchored an area of the country where environmental concerns had a greater emphasis than in most other regions of China.
- The pictures we'd seen of it were stunningly beautiful.
- It was the closest major city to the hometown of our former houseguest Huang, whom we hoped to see again.

We arrived in Guilin on a Tuesday evening and met Connie, our local guide, at the airport. She took us to our recently reconditioned hotel along one of the many small lakes and canals that thread their way through downtown Guilin. As we checked in, the hotel clerk handed us a note from Huang, whom we'd emailed from Shanghai once we knew our Guilin hotel and the dates we'd be there.

"Sorry," he'd written, "I must spend the next few days in teacher training in Chongqing. I will try to meet you for the weekend."

The following morning, Connie gave us a brief orientation to tourist Guilin, then took us by taxi to the nearby docks where cruises along the Li River begin. We enjoyed a half-day drift among baguette-shaped limestone hills and the dreamy islands and shoals that give this region a well-deserved reputation for natural beauty. Lunch was part of our tour. I noticed that the cooks and kitchen staff were careful not to throw refuse into the river. The Li River is very much a "cash cow" of the area economy and seemed to be better taken care of than most waterways in China.

Much of Guilin's downtown was being repaved. During construction, dust and/or mud predominated. Once we'd finished with the formal part of our tour, we encountered several partly finished sections while wandering on our own. Trees and shrubs had not yet been planted in future pocket gardens. They sat, drooping, their roots encased in burlap. Roadways had temporary traffic signals on rickety, barely visible poles, adding to the mayhem at major intersections.

By Friday, we'd tired of dodging showers and construction sites in rainy, torn-up downtown Guilin. We decided to stay in our room, hoping for a phone call or further message from Huang. The morning went by. No phone calls. No messages. Just as we were getting ready to slip out for a quick lunch, someone knocked at our hotel room door. We looked through the peephole into the hallway. Hurrah! There was Huang, flanked by two other men we didn't yet know.

"So good to see you again," Huang began. "Please let me introduce the headmaster of our school, Mr. Chen, and our school driver, Mr. Liu."

Over noodles and sauce at a nearby snack bar, Huang explained that he'd returned a day early from his training session to connect with us and give us a quick tour of his school. We would drive to the school and meet with most of the student body that afternoon. The trip, along a well-paved two-lane road, took about two hours.

The school was surprisingly modern, though cramped by American standards. We got a brief tour of classrooms (most set up for fifty to sixty students), student dormitories (eight students per room), administration area (with its own atrium and small indoor tropical garden), faculty apartments, and school athletic fields. Then Huang escorted us to a couple of large meeting rooms.

It had been decided that the students would have more chances to interact with the foreign guests if Jim and I each spoke with a different group. I wound up giving a brief presentation and having a question-and-answer session with the junior middle school students (equivalent to grades seven to nine in the American system), while Jim talked with the senior middle school students (grades ten to twelve). When we compared notes later, we discovered that students in both groups had asked one question that proved tricky to answer.

"Why did your bombers target our journalists?" they asked. "China is a peaceful country," they scolded.

The preceding year, NATO aircraft coordinated by the United States had bombed a Chinese embassy annex in Belgrade, Serbia. Widely decried in Chinese media, which were generally concentrated and closely controlled by the central government, the attack had resulted in three Chinese casualties. It had targeted a building that previously housed a logistics facility for the Serbian military. The only answer we had was the different version reported in American media—the bombing had been a costly and unintentional mistake based on outdated maps.

A few of the students' other questions were penetrating, if more neutral:

"Who are your heroes? Why?"

"When you were a teenager, what were your dreams for the future?"

After our side trip to Huang's hometown, we spent a couple more days in Guilin, then several days in Hong Kong—still highly vertical, still bustling, still tropical, still beautiful. Returning to Richmond, Virginia, at the end of our travels was a relief. Being surrounded mostly by native speakers of English was reassuring. It was good to get back to our house and garden. Momoyo had taken excellent care of both. We regaled her with tales of her parents and grandpa in Japan.

Around Christmas time, Jim and I were again comparing notes and sharing trip pictures with family when we had an "aha" moment. It seemed silly we hadn't noticed before—what both of us had enjoyed most, even more than the fabulous scenery, the scrumptious food, the friendships and the warm hospitality, were the two brief chances to interact with high school students in their school settings. If and when we could manage it, we would try to fulfill our dream of teaching in China, a dream that had surfaced long before when we'd first applied to the Peace Corps.

6

Early Education

初为人师。

"When you live in China as a foreigner, there are two critical moments of recognition. The first comes immediately upon arrival, when you are confronted with your own ignorance. Language, customs, history—all of it has to be learned, and the task seems impossible. Then, just as you begin to catch on, you realize that everybody else feels pretty much the same way. The place changes too fast; nobody in China has the luxury of being confident in his knowledge. Who shows a peasant how to find a factory job? How does a former Maoist learn to start a business? Who has the slightest clue how to run a car rental agency? Everything is figured out on the fly; the people are masters at improvisation. This is the second moment of recognition, and it's even more frightening than the first. Awareness of your own ignorance is a lonely feeling, but there's little consolation in sharing it with 1.3 billion neighbors."

Peter Hessler, *Strange Stones: Dispatches from East and West*, 2013.

Late 2001 found me shell-shocked and somewhat despondent. The new millennium had so far not been kind to the U.S. Although the Y2K computer meltdown some had predicted for January 1, 2000, did not occur, the terrorist attacks of September 11, 2001, produced a different kind of unease. Terrorist threats, real and imagined, took center stage, eclipsing earlier worries about local or global wars among nation-states. China and the U.S. became partial allies in the war on terror. As a long-term peace activist, I was wary of the increasing militarism among U.S. politicians. I wasn't sure how to respond.

So when a chance came to broaden my experiences with students in China, I was eager to seize the opportunity for a couple of reasons. First, I had warm recollections of the brief time I'd spent with students during our 2000 China tour. Second, I longed for a short respite from the sense of dread that had gripped much of American media and society in late 2001 and early 2002. I expected China to be less filled with the constant replaying of the Twin Towers falling in Manhattan, the constant drumbeat toward retribution.

Joan, the same American friend who'd helped arrange our 2000 tourist stay in Zhengzhou, wrote to ask me and Jim to be her temporary replacements at a foreign language school in that city where she was spending parts of one more school year. For four weeks in late March and early April she asked us to become substitute foreign English teachers. We would live and teach at the Zhengzhou International Languages College, a public-private effort to train senior high school students for further study overseas. When Joan came home for Christmas, I peppered her with questions about out duties, pay and living conditions. She reassured me on all counts.

"You'll do fine," she grinned "and I think you'll enjoy the experience."

Soon after we touched down at the Zhengzhou airport, we were welcomed by school officials with floral bouquets and ushered into a chauffeured van for our ride to the school. Being greeted as VIPs in Zhengzhou could become addictive, I realized. Once on site at ZZILC, we were escorted to the foreign teachers' guest house, shown a vacant first floor apartment where we could freshen up, then given a lunch of homemade vegetarian dumplings courtesy of the school chef. A short time later, Mr. and Mrs. Remington, an older British couple who'd taught at the school for the preceding month, came to our door to extend their welcome and to offer us their apartment upstairs for the remainder of our stay. (Because Joan had left her apartment full of her belongings and teaching materials, staying at her place was not practical.)

"We're leaving on the next plane out," Mr. Remington enlightened us. "It will be good to get back to London. We've left our place here in good form. You are welcome to some household goods we're leaving behind—we won't require them once we get back home."

As his wife looked on, Mr. Remington continued: "I hope your stay will be more pleasant, now that the weather is warming." I later learned that he'd been sidelined by a serious attack of bronchitis for part of his chilly month in Zhengzhou.

Their offer was especially welcome. The second floor was an ideal location in this three-story Foreign Teachers' Apartment Building, less susceptible than the first floor to the occasional flash floods that had ruined some of Joan's belongings during her previous teaching assignment. It was also partially shielded by the third floor from correspondingly leaky roofs. Because of the Remingtons' generosity, we would begin our stay well stocked with bedding, towels, laundry supplies, and kitchen equipment.

"Thank you so much," I told him. "I wish we could have more time to get to know you both. I wish you safe travels home." Soon afterward, the Remingtons took their leave.

After a short meeting with Shannon, the school's Foreign Affairs Officer, Jim and I returned to the Foreign Teachers' Apartment Building and began to explore the apartment the Remingtons had left us. It consisted of four rooms: a large living room with a kitchen area along one edge, a bedroom, an office, and a bathroom. It came equipped with room heaters in the living room and bedroom, an electric rice cooker, an electric wok, a television, a sofa and two armchairs with panda-patterned throws over their upholstery, an office desk and chair, and a computer with (sometimes slow) internet access. Its plumbing included a kitchen sink, a small washing machine, plus another sink and a sit toilet in a mostly Chinese-style bathroom. The bathroom walls and floor were covered in tiles, with a drain in the middle of the room for run-off from the unenclosed shower. Our bedroom had a big, comfortable bed piled high with lots of quilts.

Joan may not have told us, or we may not have been paying attention, but we didn't realize until sometime after our arrival that the school and its campus were brand new that academic year. Buildings and a small sports yard had been rapidly constructed of concrete, tile and brick within an enclosing wall. The campus lay just inside the third ring road at the northern edge of the city. The school was an experiment. Its curriculum, outreach, and schedule shifted frequently.

We would teach several classes of intermediate and advanced conversational English to on-site students of roughly high school age, a few as old as twenty. Most came from newly wealthy families. None were eligible for entrance to any of China's most prestigious universities. On the standardized college entrance test administered all over China every June, some of our students had gotten scores too low to qualify for a good school. Others had not even bothered to take the test. These students' parents had opted to send them to ZZILC to help give them the alternative of studying abroad—for this they would need money, which was generally not a problem. What *was* a problem was that they'd also need acceptable scores on either the American-based TOEFL (Test of English as a Foreign Language) or the British-based IELTS (International English Language Testing System) to be accepted at a foreign university.

Few Chinese teachers of English in Zhengzhou had been exposed to either the TOEFL or the IELTS. Traditional Chinese teaching methods meshed poorly with the types of questions the students would be expected to answer. Especially challenging was the conversational component of the IELTS. All of us—students, Chinese staff, and foreign teachers—were on a steep learning curve in foreign language education.

The seventy or so ZZILC daytime students were nearly all Henan-bred "little emperors" or "little empresses"—only children born in the wake of China's one child policy. They had for much of their lives been coddled materially by indulgent parents and grandparents. They were now, for better or worse, the sole carriers of their families' hopes and dreams. As such, these teens were under tremendous family pressure to succeed and to make their elders proud. Often, they had had little previous personal experience or training in dealing with adversity.

In retrospect, I'm guessing that school officials spent a good bit of their time on recruitment, persuading families to fork over the substantial ZZILC tuition so that their children would have a leg up toward success in a rapidly changing China. This new China sometimes must have baffled older generations of Chinese nearly as much as it baffled us.

Among the ZZILC day students, most of the boys were more interested in pick-up basketball games on the one truncated outdoor court than in indoor study. Most of the girls were somewhat interested in the boys, but mainly interested in shopping, cosmetics and fashion. I started my substitute stint by using materials the school gave us, but gradually branched out to include more basketball, fashion, and shopping terms.

School principal Jiang used his extensive network of contacts to create varied earning opportunities for the school. The principal's wife, Mrs. Li, though without any official title, served in many unofficial capacities: mentor, nurse, social secretary, hostess, and purchasing agent for materials the foreign teachers might need for our housekeeping and teaching. Along with the other teachers, school staff included a recently hired assistant principal to help enforce discipline and to establish standards of cleanliness in the dorms. Shannon, the Foreign Affairs Officer, handled the visas and paperwork for foreign teachers while she practiced her English with us as often as she could, preparing herself for any opportunities that might later develop with the foreign-based companies beginning to move into the area.

Zhengzhou was at an awkward stage, partway between traditional and modern. One day early in our stay, we started out on an afternoon walk in the vicinity of the school. Several "bread box" taxis were parked by the school entrance. These small light-weight minivans, usually colored yellow, provided much of the personalized transportation in Zhengzhou in 2002. They were not very safe, but were more sheltered and faster than bicycles or walking. A couple of taxi drivers gestured for us to get in. We waved them off and continued our stroll.

A block or two later, we saw a donkey cart come trotting by on a side road, the first animal-powered vehicle we'd noticed in town. A local junk collector was perched on a bench at the front of the cart, which was piled high with cast-off clothes and rags. He occasionally used a light flick of his whip to urge his donkey forward, all the while carrying on an extended conversation on his cell phone. The juxtaposition of donkey cart and cell phone at first startled and amused me.

Then I began to realize that modes of transportation and modes of communication in Zhengzhou meshed in different ways from what I was used to. Private cars were still expensive and rare. Road infrastructure, though being built out at a frantic pace, was hugely uneven, ranging from a few state-of-the-art expressways near major cities to rutted narrow dirt tracks in much of the countryside. Pragmatic Chinese used whatever means of transportation were available, affordable, and appropriate—draft animals, bicycles, tricycles, motorcycles, small tractors, buses, taxis, farm equipment, and handcarts. Similarly, once cell phones became available, Chinese communications enterprises, never having strung much cabling for land lines, rapidly constructed national networks of cell phone towers and began manufacturing inexpensive cell phones. Even rag pickers carried them.

After our first day of teaching, Jim and I made a foray to Zhengzhou's largest department store to pick up additional household and teaching supplies. The arrangement of merchandise and the absence of English signage mystified us. We went begging to the principal's wife for help, which Mrs. Li graciously provided.

After a few more days at ZZILC's main campus, we learned from the school administration that we would teach auxiliary lessons elsewhere. We were asked to hold enrichment classes for students in several successive area public high schools, including the one where Joan had taught previously. I quickly developed a couple of repeatable lessons for these encounters, including a short history of Chinese immigration to the United States. I would explain that the first large-scale Chinese settlement in America came in the wake of the 1848 discovery of gold in California. During the following decade, several thousand Chinese young men crossed the Pacific to "Old Gold Mountain," one of the Chinese names for the city of San Francisco.

I used simple tools to help connect the students to these Chinese-American pioneers. I drew a rough outline map of the U.S. and its relationship to the Pacific Ocean, pointing out that California was across the Pacific from China's east coast. On the chalkboard I also wrote the first verse and chorus of the American folk song "Clementine," with its vocabulary about "miners" and "49ers." I wanted to give the students a sense of the hardships those early miners and area settlers endured, whatever their origins. After I sang the excerpt a couple of times, I encouraged the students to sing along. Most did, picking up the tune immediately.

At the end of our singing, several students looked puzzled. Resigned to not knowing what had intrigued them, I expected them to sit quietly, as I'd seen the students doing when I'd attended sample lessons at Joan's prior school. So I was pleasantly surprised when one of the bolder students raised his hand. I called on him. He stood by his desk, shuffling just a little.

"Excuse me, Teacher," he began. "We all know that tune, but it has different words."

"How interesting," I managed. "Would you and your friends be willing to teach me the Chinese words?" I enunciated slowly.

It took a little while for the students to settle down and begin their "teach the teacher" lesson. The student I'd called on coached me on the Chinese lyrics, which, he explained, meant "Happy New Year"—"*Xinnian Hao.*" As I got closer to the correct pronunciation, several of his cohorts joined in. By the end of the lesson, we could sing fairly close equivalents to both the "Clementine" verse and

"*Xinnian Hao*," whose mutual tune, like other simple folk tunes, had crossed the Pacific at least once.

During our second week, we began giving conversational English lessons two evenings a week to adult learners at a facility nearer the city center. Our evening students, professionals in their twenties, thirties, or forties, were tired at the end of their long work days. They were also much more knowledgeable about the world than our day students, and considerably more enthusiastic. One man was a manager at a local television station. Another was a chemical engineer. A woman student clerked at a local branch of the Bank of China. Another administered sonograms for wealthy expectant Chinese couples. As we got to know these students better, we branched out from the initial conversation prompts we'd gotten from ZZILC.

"Tell us about Americans' spending habits," one requested.

"What are your favorite foods? How often do you eat in restaurants?"

"How much do you pay in taxes? How often?"

"What is American television really like?" asked the TV station manager.

We noticed a divide between the older workers, whose careers had been dictated by the government, and the younger ones, who'd had to find their own placements in China's increasingly freewheeling economy.

During our month of teaching, my first experience in the classroom in over thirty years, I regained a deep appreciation for the level of effort put in by many teachers in whatever culture—having "summers off" seemed almost a sanity requirement after the hectic pace of my Zhengzhou teaching.

Western Easter occurred while Jim and I were in Zhengzhou.

"Aha," I thought, "an intercultural teaching opportunity!"

I scoured the city's markets and stores for the more secular accoutrements of this springtime festival with help and advice from Mrs. Li. Zhengzhou's poshest foreign tourist hotel had a big display of bunnies and colored eggs and one of the city's parks had temporary booths where

Easter decorations were sold. After several shopping expeditions, I'd scrounged up jelly beans and chocolate bunnies, plus fabric, poster paper, glue, staples, and fake flowers to make Easter bonnets. The foreign teachers' Sunday afternoon Easter social drew many of our students plus some Chinese teachers as well.

"Many American towns," I explained, "hold afternoon Easter parades. Everyone is glad when the weather turns pleasant after the chill of winter. People dress in their finest spring clothes, including elaborate flowered hats for the women. Sometimes they bring their dogs along and put costumes on them, too. In our town, people walk up and down a big street called Monument Avenue, showing off their fine outfits and greeting their neighbors."

Some of our teen girl students crafted elaborate flowered hats of their own. The most chic pretended that our room's center aisle was a fashion runway. Some English was spoken if the conversation rarely moved beyond the level of "Nice hat!" All the candy and snacks were consumed.

The substantial minority of ZZILC's on-site students who came from out of town boarded at school dorms during the week. The most-distant (and wealthiest) students came from far enough away so going home on a standard weekend was impractical. Therefore, teaching schedules at ZZILC were adjusted to give both students and staff alternate Fridays off. This made students' separations from family less lengthy and also gave staff some three-day weekends. Just before our first such break, Shannon took us aside.

"Principal Jiang would like to take the foreign teachers on an excursion tomorrow," she told us. "Please be ready at the front entrance of the Foreign Teachers' Apartment Building at 8 a.m."

The day started out foggy, so the carful of us—Principal Jiang, who drove, British foreign teacher Eliza, Shannon, Jim and I—took secondary roads to the ancient capital city of Kaifeng, not wanting to risk an accident on the area's high-speed expressway. A city has been on the Kaifeng site for at least two millennia, periodically abandoned, then rebuilt, as dynasties came and went. Kaifeng's heyday was during the eleventh century, when it was a leading trade center at the junction of four important canals. Positioned astride the Yellow River, Kaifeng also suffered from periodic floods. The incarnation we saw on our brief visit consisted of replicas of parts of the city at its most prosperous a thousand years ago—like Colonial Williamsburg, perhaps, but with a *lot* more history.

Principal Jiang escorted us first to a tourist highlight: a monument to an incorruptible local official from long ago. We lunched at a famous dumpling restaurant, downing six or seven trays of differently flavored steamed dumplings. After lunch, at a different tourist area, Eliza paid a small fee to be trotted around the town square in a traditional wedding sedan chair, a red-curtained enclosure carried on poles by four strapping young Chinese men.

By late afternoon, when it was time to return to school, visibility had improved. Principal Jiang risked the school car on the high-speed expressway, returning in about half the time of our two-hour outbound journey.

The weekend just before our departure, we accepted invitations to meals at two students' area homes. The closer dwelling, within walking distance, was that of a beautiful young woman whose parents had relocated to Zhengzhou from Inner Mongolia several years earlier. Annette, her mother, and her aunt had prepared a delicious lunch. We ate in an outdoor courtyard behind their kitchen. They'd built a trellis with an overhanging arbor that was especially beautiful in early spring. Language was a bit of a problem, but we were able to share some fabulous weather while spearing and eating as many slithery, delicious lamb dumplings as we could stuff ourselves with, and later slurping a clear broth soup.

The other home was the country estate of a young man, Blue, whose family had amassed a small fortune doing road construction and paving. Blue's father sent a car and driver to pick us up at school. The family mansion, situated beside a levee along the Yellow River, was enclosed by a wrought iron fence, its circular driveway guarded by stylized stone lions on either side of the front gate. The house itself was two stories, with a tiled roof, a tiled exterior, and several large Greek-style columns across its front, an architectural hodgepodge that reminded me ever so slightly of *Gone With the Wind's* "Tara." The ground floor, the only part of the house we saw inside, had several large sitting rooms and a bathroom whose Western-style bathtub was apparently used mostly for washing vegetables.

While Blue's mother prepared a feast, Blue and his father took us for a stroll through a nearby hamlet. Blue sometimes consulted his electronic dictionary for the English name of a local landmark. As we headed back toward the family compound, a local elder greeted us. After chatting with Blue and his father, the man entertained us with a spirited rendition of several Chinese songs, undaunted by his lack of all but two teeth.

"Henan-style Chinese opera," Blue informed us proudly.

Blue's mom had made several vegetable dishes, a main dish with pork, and an abundance of dumplings.

From our first, jet-lagged meal in Zhengzhou to our final send-off feast, most festive occasions included large quantities of Chinese dumplings, variously called *jiaozi* or *baozi*. These steamed or fried relatives of the wontons available in most Chinese-American restaurants are a taste I first developed during my time at ZZILC. Fillings were most often a mixture of pork and vegetables. For those whose faith, health, or environmental sensitivities excluded pork, dumplings were available with lamb, tofu or a hearty vegetable mix as the base. *Jaiozi* are small and crescent shaped, with thin skins and fluted edges, while *baozi* are larger, doughier, rounded, gathered at the top in puckers. Whenever and wherever I encounter the scent of dumplings steaming, it brings back lots of happy memories. A good dumpling feast is still one of my favorite meals.

7

Living in the White House

奉为上宾。

"'I dreamed about Kweilin (Guilin) before I ever saw it,' my mother began, speaking Chinese. 'I dreamed of jagged peaks lining a curving river, with magic moss greening the banks. At the tops of these peaks were white mists. And if you could float down this river and eat the moss for food, you would be strong enough to climb the peak. If you slipped, you would only fall into a bed of soft moss and laugh. And once you reached the top, you would be able to see everything and feel such happiness it would be enough to never have worries in your life ever again.'"

Amy Tan, *The Joy Luck Club*, 1989.

My chance to live in the White House came and went during the spring of 2004. I was not a guest of a U.S. President. Rather, I was sharing a tiny apartment with my husband Jim in the city of Guilin in southern China. A friend of a friend had arranged for us to do a short-term teaching stint at a large middle school there, in a different part of the city than what we'd seen as tourists in 2000. In 2003, while I'd been tied up with business matters in the U.S., Jim had come to China without me for a month. He'd taught at Mr. Huang's school in a small Guangxi town, traveled nearby, and thoroughly enjoyed himself. He wanted a similar opportunity at a different school for 2004. On reflection, I decided I'd enjoyed our 2002 experiences in Zhengzhou enough to be willing to give teaching in China a second try. So here we were, in a post-industrial area of Guilin that housed and employed working-class Chinese. Our school hosts had gone all out to make our lodgings comfortable and attractive, including putting a fresh coat of whitewash on our apartment's exterior front wall. Ours was the middle unit in a building of five adjacent single-story apartments. The others, their front walls still dingy gray cement, housed unmarried Chinese staff members. I think the local teachers enjoyed the irony of our place's nickname as much as we did.

No foreign teachers had ever been to Guilin Number 4 Middle School before. In addition to the whitewash, adaptations for our comfort included a heavy metal front door with a padlock, and metal bars on the single window at the back of our unit. We never figured out whether our neighborhood in Guilin was unsafe or whether our hosts had watched too many U.S.-based crime dramas and decided we'd be jittery without the extra safety features. None of the other apartments had such security enhancements. All the units, though, had patched tile roofs, ours just as thoroughly patched as everyone else's.

Our neighborhood might or might not have been safe, but it was certainly noisy. We seemed to be on the flight path for military jets doing practice runs from a nearby air base. A couple of buildings away, just outside the school's front gate, a major road widening project was underway, causing the same mixture of mud and cacophony we'd encountered four years earlier when the tourist area was getting a makeover.

We hoped during this year's China visit to get more chances to mix with the local population. With luck, we might even get exposure to other ethnic groups, since the area surrounding Guilin was officially not a province but the "Guangxi Zhuang Autonomous Region," named for the Zhuang, the most populous of several minority groups.

We arrived late on a Thursday afternoon. We had the luxury of several days to adjust to our new time zone and new surroundings before starting to teach the following Monday. After an evening welcome banquet and a time-zone-shifted night's sleep, we spent Friday getting further acquainted with our apartment, school schedules, and household routines.

The White House had one livable room plus a small bathroom and an entrance hallway. In addition to our double bed, the main room contained a school desk, a chair, a lamp, a small refrigerator, and a freestanding space heater. The heater was circular, about eighteen inches across, with rings of heating coils around a central hub. It looked a bit like an oversized toaster, and we actually used it as such. Our entrance hallway had some glass-fronted cabinets with shelves for storage.

The bathroom shoe-horned in a small washing machine, a squat toilet, and a shower with a flexible hose that could also be used to flush the toilet or fill the washer when we did laundry. Someone had alerted the school administration about sit toilets, so we had a metal-framed fold-out "throne" chair, a little like an elder's walker, that we could place over the toilet hole when our muscles required additional support.

Once we'd completed our inventory of apartment amenities, we explored the surrounding neighborhood and did some rudimentary shopping. We'd been surprised by the chill in the weather—it was late March, but this was southern China. Wasn't it supposed to be subtropical? Luckily, our hosts had included the space heater and a warm quilt for our bed with our initial supply of household goods. I bought a padded jacket that would fit me (extra-large in Chinese sizes). Jim got an additional sweater, also extra-large. Problem solved.

Before we even met our first class, we got a chance for a weekend field trip, organized by our former houseguest, Mr. Huang. Huang had previously taught several of the younger English teachers at Number 4 Middle School. Once he knew we'd be teaching there, he persuaded the school administration to subsidize an initial weekend trip for these new foreign guests to a scenic area in the hills north of Guilin—the Dragon's Backbone (*Longji*) rice terraces in Longsheng County. Huang would go along with us as our translator. One of his cousins would provide a car and chauffeur services.

The main scenic village was about a two-hour drive from Guilin. We made plenty of intermediate stops along the way. The early part of our journey used a limited access toll road, not crowded on a Saturday morning. As we got higher into the hills, we followed a series of secondary roads, after a while paralleling a mountain stream.

At the entrance to one small village, our driver stopped the car and we all got out. We were quickly surrounded by a group of short, slender women wearing ethnic costumes. Most had buns of shining black hair piled atop their heads. Huang explained to us in English that these women were part of the Yao minority, a group concentrated in the more mountainous areas of Guangxi. The women escorted us across a swinging footbridge over the stream into the main part of their village. Once we'd arrived at a sort of small town square, they pulled out baskets full of cloth pieces and began showing us the hand embroidery that was a local specialty. We asked Huang to translate our regret at not being in a good position to make purchases.

"Foreigners just arrived in China. Not time yet to buy souvenirs. Car is small, very crowded. Not buy cloth, though very beautiful."

With Huang's help, we worked out an alternate deal to everyone's satisfaction. We were fascinated by the women's embroidered costumes and elaborate hairdos. Huang had told us that women in this ethnic group were immensely proud of their long hair, which they often left uncut until old age. We asked if we could pay the women for the privilege of photographing them in their costumes, some of them with their hair down.

"No problem," Huang assured us.

Several of the more mature women removed lots of pins and combs, letting out tresses that came to their knees. They then posed coquettishly for our cameras.

After a couple more stops for snacks and rest breaks, we arrived at the busiest area of Longji. The rice terraces were breathtaking, in some places snaking their way along slopes that seemed too steep even for mountain goats. Each terrace was perhaps three to four feet wide, usually separated from the ones above and below by low ledges of local stone. This early in the season, many had been planted with rapeseed, an oil-bearing plant whose spikes of yellow blossoms can light up even the dreariest landscape. Area houses were made of wood, three stories tall, with hand-hewn beams and elaborately carved doors, windows, and shutters. Several minority groups in addition to the Zhuang make their homes in Guangxi, including the Yao, the Dong, and the Miao.

The main tourist area had lots of souvenir and craft shops, plus a substantial snack bar where we ate a noodle lunch alongside a busload of Swedes and their tour guide. In early afternoon, we walked along stone-lined paths among the terraces. Most had been constructed by hand over several centuries starting a millennium ago and had been meticulously maintained since their completion.

During our walk, Huang stopped several times to check for cell phone coverage. Once he found a good spot, he stepped aside and made some calls. About mid-afternoon, we returned to our car and rode further into the hills to the edge of Longsheng Hot Springs National Forest Park. Huang had decided that we could afford to spend the night nearby before returning to school on Sunday. He'd determined by phone that the hotels at the hot springs were a better bargain than those at the terraces and could accept foreigners. An added attraction was the availability of bathing pools with water piped in from nearby springs. We shared a supper of chicken, local vegetables, and more noodles at the hotel restaurant. Jim and I had trouble keeping our eyes open, and soon retired to our room. Huang and his cousin switched into swim trunks and tried out the local pools.

The following morning, the four of us saw one of the rare forests in this part of China, along with more mountain streams. We sighted a local species of wild monkey from a distance, across a wooded ravine. By midday, we were back at school. Huang's cousin made his farewells. Huang found a nearby noodle shop where we three ate lunch. Then he left us to finish our preparations for Monday's classes.

As we got introduced to the Chinese teachers of English and learned something about our schedules, we formed the decided impression that our role would be mainly as window dressing: schools in less developed areas of China sometimes used the presence of foreign teachers as a marketing tool to attract more students. Number 4 Middle was across the Li River from the tourist portion of Guilin, in an area that was gradually being converted from heavy industry to a mix of technical schools, shops, and smaller factories. The school had about two thousand students in grades seven through twelve. Some were day students from other parts of Guilin or the nearby countryside. Others came from further away and boarded at the school. Perhaps half a mile down the area's major street was Seven Star Park, a large expanse of greenery dotted with limestone hills and caves. Once the road repaving and widening was complete, access to the park would be greatly improved.

We started our Guilin teaching stint with minimal computer access. The White House had neither a computer nor the space for one. The few machines at the school's administrative offices were very slow and typically oversubscribed, as we'd learned shortly after our arrival when we wanted to send a brief "got here safe" email back to the U.S. Having become accustomed to internet access during our Zhengzhou stay, we'd expected to be able to stay in fairly frequent email contact with family and friends in the U.S. Also, Jim liked to use internet research to bolster his presentations. What to do?

We phoned Teacher Huang.

"Where can we get internet access that's faster and less busy than the school office computers?" Jim asked.

"I think we can find internet bars near your school," Huang told him. "I'll learn which is best and take you there after we meet for dinner tomorrow night."

The preferred internet bar, it turned out, was an easy walk down a back alley, maybe a couple hundred yards from the school gate. In 2004, most Chinese in Guangxi did not yet have home computers, so internet bars were quite popular especially with students. Charges by the minute were relatively inexpensive. Whenever Jim went to check email or do internet research, he was at least a generation older than most other customers. After a while, the proprietor recognized Jim and no longer asked for his school ID.

Our four weeks of teaching would be spread out among most of the students so that we'd spend only two or three sessions with any one class, not enough time to get to know the students or to impart much information. Jim would interact with the older students, tenth and eleventh graders, while I worked with the seventh and eighth graders. We were told that the ninth and the twelfth graders were too busy for whatever enrichment activities we might provide. At the time, we did not understand the reasons for this. We'd gotten used to hearing "too busy" from Chinese colleagues, even when being busy was not really a factor. Most Chinese people we knew would go to great lengths to avoid having to respond to a request with an outright "no." "Too busy" was a frequent stand-in.

In subsequent teaching stints, we learned that the final years of junior middle school (ninth grade) and senior middle school (twelfth grade) could be a living hell for both teachers and students. During those years, especially twelfth grade, everyone involved in the education process really *was* too busy. Students got very little sleep, staying up until the wee hours studying and doing homework. Teachers were under tremendous pressure to have their students perform well on standardized tests. At the end of ninth grade, such tests determined students' eligibility for further high school—those with the lowest scores would end their formal education. These early school leavers typically could look forward to nothing better than a minimum wage job as a greeter at a China-based Walmart or near equivalent. At the end of twelfth grade, students wanting to go on for higher education had to take the universally dreaded "*gao kao*" (big test), a nationally standardized test whose results would determine students' college chances and choices.

By the end of our first week of teaching, we'd figured out that it was more convenient and pleasant between class sessions to hang out in the English teachers' workroom rather than to slog back and forth to our apartment at the far edge of campus. The teachers' workroom gave us chances to get to know some of the twenty other English teachers better and also to get more glimpses into the Chinese education system. We looked over the shoulders of teachers we'd gotten to know as they prepared lessons or graded students' notebooks. We asked questions about the materials they were using and the techniques they relied on to check their students' understanding. Much of the work was rote. Class sizes were large. Some teachers expressed frustrations similar to ones we'd had as parents of students in our American high school system.

"Too many tests," exclaimed young Miss Liang, one of Teacher Huang's former students, as she graded still another set of quizzes.

A little later, Mr. He shrugged. "This answer key makes no sense. It says that choice B is the only correct answer, but it's identical to choice D. How can one be right and not the other?"

Most of the Chinese teachers of English were in their twenties. Partway through our stay, Miss Liang, along with her college roommate Miss Yang, invited us for a weekend stay in the countryside. We'd visit some tourist sites and spend an overnight with Miss Yang's family at their home in a citrus-growing region of Guangxi. This particular weekend in early April turned out to be the "*Qing Ming* (Tomb Sweeping) Festival," an occasion when many Chinese returned briefly to their hometowns to clean and beautify the graves of their ancestors.

Over the course of the weekend, we rode in buses, minibuses, and taxis. We straddled motorcycles. We poled bamboo boats. We visited an ersatz "traditional village," and what seemed to be a genuine, if somewhat decrepit, small shrine honoring Confucius. We luxuriated in the scent of the orange blossoms, while occasionally choking on exhaust fumes or pesticide residues. We learned that the Yangs' acre of intensely cultivated orchard and vegetable garden was much more typical of Chinese farm plots than the mega-acreage monoculture farms we'd grown accustomed to in the U.S. As Sunday afternoon began, we thanked our host family for their hospitality. With considerable guidance from Miss Yang, we found a more direct route back to Guilin in a rather crowded van.

Most of our teaching focused on getting the students to practice English pronunciation and intonation and to expand their English vocabularies. I found that using simple tunes provided one way to bridge the gap between tonal Mandarin and "atonal" English. Guilin's weather was rainy. I wracked my brain for songs about rainy weather, and eventually came up with a few: "It's Raining, It's Pouring"; "Singin' in the Rain"; "Raindrops Keep Fallin' on My Head"; and "April Showers" (most of our stay occurred during April).

One morning during our second week, as I was dodging yet another shower and looking for a vacant cubicle in the workroom, I hummed a few bars of "Rhythm of the Rain," a sappy teen love song from the American 1960s. I'd heard an instrumental version of the tune played over the school loudspeakers the day before. Another teacher, Ms. Gao, came up to me, smiling. She and her theater-director husband lived off-campus in a new downtown apartment she'd shown off to us the previous weekend.

"Thank you again for the CD of American jazz," she began. "We really enjoy playing it on our new entertainment center. I noticed you humming the tune to 'Rhythm of the Rain'," she continued. "I have a recording of the Deng Li-Jun version. (Deng was a Taiwanese singer whose ballads and love songs first were allowed in mainland China as the country intensified its period of reform and opening.) It's a beautiful song, and her voice is so delicate. Perhaps you'd like to come listen some evening."

I didn't get the chance for a repeat visit to Ms. Gao's apartment, but I later learned from a Chinese-American friend that Chinese students of her 1980s generation used to gauge the relative openness of government policies by whether or not Ms. Deng's songs were allowed to be played on state radio.

Near the end of our stay, our school principal invited us to a banquet with other members of the English faculty. Two full tables of us would eat at a special staff dining room, separate from the standard dining hall. Most of the meal contained familiar dishes, including some specialties of the local area: a pork and taro casserole, some fried tofu squares, braised river fish, lots of local greens, even some crispy duck. We thought we were ending our meal when trays of fruit were brought out. In the usual sequence, the next step would have been passing around toothpicks so we could cover our mouths with one hand while discreetly using the toothpick in the other hand to pick out any lingering shreds of meat, vegetables or fruit. However, one of the chefs then brought out some more plates, these full of what looked sort of like chocolate croissants. Sweet desserts are unusual in China. I wondered what these were. Several of the other teachers helped themselves, but I held back at first.

"Try one," urged Mrs. Li, an older English teacher who'd befriended us. She lived in an apartment building across from the White House with her doctor husband and teenaged son. "I think you'll like it."

The pastry was crunchy and sweet, with layers of crisp dough and a slightly nutty-flavored filling. It would have been rude to take two, but I really liked the taste.

"It's delicious," I admitted. "Do you know what's in the filling?"

"It's a special kind of ant, fried to bring out the flavor and crispness," Mrs. Li explained. "They're a bit hard to find in the markets, and somewhat expensive, so we don't have them very often. We thought they would be a good treat for our foreign guests."

As our 2004 Guilin stay ended, I was happy I'd given teaching in China another chance. The students at Guilin Number 4 Middle were not tremendously advanced in their English studies, but they were less jaded and more enthusiastic than the day students we'd dealt with in Zhengzhou. I was getting better at finding ways to help students practice their pronunciation without making it a big chore. In addition to our interactions with students and staff, we'd had a weekend chance, with Huang's help, to travel to a more natural, "wilder" areas of China that would have been inaccessible to us earlier: the forest park near Longsheng with its monkeys. We even had our first glimpse of pandas in habitats within their natural range, as I'll describe at length in the next chapter.

8

Forest Preserves, Pools, Pandas, and Beaches- Nature in China

华夏如此多娇。

Giant Panda Protection Network for 3 Million Ha (7.5 million acres) of Habitat
With the help of the Chinese government a giant panda protection Network has
been set up. This protection network consists of 62 nature reserves, and a couple of
forest farms, migration corridors, and sustainably managed forests. It covers 57
percent of giant panda habitat and 71 percent of its population in the wild.

(T)he giant panda protection network is the first protected area network for
wildlife in China, and has played a very important role in safeguarding a viable
population of giant pandas . . . With a location in the upper reaches of the
Yangtze, this network has also benefited . . . hundreds of other key animals and
plants . . . as well as hundreds of millions of people in this region.
　　World Wildlife Fund China, *http://en.wwfchina.org/en/what_we_do/species/,*
accessed August 22, 2017.

Initially my impressions of China, from a distance and then up closer, focused on its human artifacts: historical monuments, intricate carvings and calligraphy, huge cities, intensely cultivated farmlands, immense construction projects, and a continuous written history covering several thousand years. Though I've grown to respect the depth and scope of the country's rich cultural heritage, it's been my chances to see more of its relatively wild areas that have most drawn me to cherish this sometimes harsh, often stunning land. Starting in 2004, I began to experience more of China's natural wonders, first through more thorough explorations of Guilin and its surroundings, then via chances to venture further into parts of China less impacted by humans. I also started to realize how important, even crucial, China's natural features have been in shaping its culture over time—China contains some of the world's highest mountains, some of its vastest deserts. China has surging river systems prone to flooding. It contains active earthquake zones, long coastlines, and unique exotic species.

Near the end of our Guilin teaching stint in 2004, I asked my Chinese colleagues for advice: What was the most beautiful natural area I could visit in China during a week's travel? Because students would be busy taking standardized tests in late April, our active teaching time had gotten truncated—we'd have a free week before our outbound flights back to the U.S. The area around Guilin was itself quite stunning, its limestone hills rising steeply from meandering streams in valleys where emerald rice paddies alternated with pastures of grazing water buffalo. However, this immediate area still bore a heavy human imprint. I was looking for a place of natural beauty further afield, maybe even wilderness, Chinese style.

"How about Tibet?" someone suggested. "We hear it has beautiful mountains, and its spiritual heritage sets it apart from the rest of China."

The expense and logistics were too challenging—it was nearly at the other end of the country. The only practical way to get there would be by plane, via a long, expensive set of flights. In addition, most of the Tibet Autonomous Region was at high altitude, with air so thin that many visitors from lowland regions developed breathing problems.

Then other colleagues told me about Jiuzhaigou and Huanglong, two outstanding natural areas in northern Sichuan province. One of our Chinese friends helped find an inexpensive China-based touring company and then helped me and Jim book airline, hotel and tour tickets. We'd fly to Sichuan's capital city of Chengdu to join a China Youth Travel Services four-day/three-night group bus tour to two of China's earliest-established national parks. Once our park visits were over, we'd have a few days to explore Chengdu and its surroundings before heading home.

Both Jiuzhaigou and Huanglong are at a high altitude, though not as high as most of Tibet. Each park has sets of interlocking travertine pools, made over centuries by the slow buildup of "lips" of calcium carbonate, the same chemical compound that forms stalactites and stalagmites in caves. Jiuzhaigou's main features were the crystal clear lakes and the cascades large and small formed behind travertine dams. The area, whose Chinese name means "nine village valley," had long been a grazing and logging area for ethnic Tibetans. Starting in the late 1970s, it was turned into parkland, with sections of it reforested. Huanglong got both its landscape and its name (Yellow Dragon) from the long serpentine slopes of travertine. Huanglong is bordered by trails, with a fire-tower-like overlook you can climb up to get a broader view of the breathtaking landscape.

As our tour bus reached a plateau area on the way to the parks, the driver stopped to let us stretch our legs. I saw blinding white snow banks near the sides of the road, unlike the dingy bare earth or straggly grasses in open areas of more settled China. It took our bus driver almost thirteen hours to navigate the often twisting mountain roads between Chengdu and Jiuzhaigou. By the time we actually arrived at the tourist village near the park's entrance, it was well after dark. Our guide spoke little English. I caught a few Chinese expressions, but was not entirely clear about plans for the following day. A younger man who'd sat across the aisle from us on the bus came up and provided some English translation.

"Guide says we all breakfast together at Sheraton Hotel tomorrow morning at seven," he explained. "Then we get on electric bus for day-long tour in park. You get your own lunch. By evening, back to Sheraton for buffet dinner and then local performers."

Once at Jiuzhaigou, I looked down through the clear, deep water of its larger lakes. Even in the deepest of them, submerged objects showed in minute detail. Near an overlook above beautiful Panda Lake, I was able to grab a few precious moments of solitude away from the crowds of other eager tourists. Later, near the furthest point along the bus loop, I took a short trail through stands of old growth trees. Only a few squirrels watched as I gazed upward through the branches of conifers several times my age. The following day's itinerary, over a high mountain pass and on to Huanglong, had stunning vistas of snow-capped mountains, but I missed the groves of ancestral trees, the sense of reverence I'd experienced at Jiuzhaigou.

In 2004, no petroleum-powered vehicles were allowed inside either park. At Jiuzhaigou, electric buses made continuous loops, with well-marked pick-up and drop-off points. At Huanglong, hiking or human-hefted sedan chairs were the locomotion modes of choice. I was very grateful for the chance to visit both parks. I said a small prayer that we hordes of tourists, hungry for natural beauty, would not, as hordes of tourists are wont to do, love these parks to death.

A few days after our Sichuan parks trip, I first got to see semi-wild pandas. Few people have seen these reclusive animals in their natural setting, as panda populations now likely number only in the low thousands across the entire span of their dwindling range. Seeing them in something close to their natural habitat was our best bet. Back in Chengdu at our tourist hotel, I hired a driver/guide to take us to the Wolong Giant Panda Preserve and back as a day trip.

We'd heard about the reserve through various publications of the World Wildlife Fund, for whom the cuddly-looking bear has become a symbol. When we ventured there in spring 2004, road conditions in less traveled parts of Sichuan were iffy. After nearly four hours in the car, some of it down muddy narrow roads with intermittent pavement, we reached the area where we expected the reserve to be. I'd almost given up on finding it when I spotted a sign at the left of the road near the top of a small rise: "Wolong National Nature Reserve," it said, welcoming visitors in both Chinese and English. Starting in 1963, international wildlife organizations such as WWF began partnering with the Chinese government at this center in efforts to stabilize or even increase endangered panda populations.

"We've finally arrived!" I laughed with a mixture of joy and relief.

Our driver heard my English-language jabbering, and noticed the sign, too. He slowed still further, then coasted down one final slope toward the entry gate and a small parking area.

At the park entrance, the driver conversed with park officials to negotiate our entrance fees, then finger-wrote the figure on his hand for us to see. I don't remember the price, but it was a lot less than we were paying for a whole day of being chauffeured around the Chinese countryside. We paid our fees, plus his, too. We were among only a few visitors. I listened carefully as one of the senior scientists led us to the first set of panda enclosures and started explaining parts of their program in halting English.

"Some pandas in cages," he said for our benefit, showing us through a series of zoo-like masonry "pandapartments."

"We monitor pandas, feed them, check when females are fertile." Although birth rates at the center were rather low, he was proud that at least a few panda cubs had been born here.

Further up the hill were several large areas enclosed by high open-weave metal fences. In the first enclosure we came to, an older male had worn the grassy vegetation near the fence down to a bare earth path. He paced from one side of the enclosure to the other, occasionally pausing to stand on his hind legs and peer out through the fence; then he resumed his vigil: back and forth, back and forth.

Next, we came to a juvenile playground that had equipment even human children might envy—a nifty combination of ropes, ladders, inclines, and mounted wooden platforms. There, seven panda cubs tussled and pawed at each other, playing their version of "king of the mountain."

In the most remote public part of the reserve we discovered some even larger enclosures, hardly distinguishable from the landscape around them.

"We prepare some pandas to return to wild," the scientist told us. Rather than being furnished with pre-cut bamboo, the pre-release pandas had to learn to forage for themselves, harvesting bamboo from stands within their enclosures. The first pre-release panda was still about a year from the end of his three-year acclimatization period. By the time of his release, he'd have been fitted with a radio collar to enable park personnel to track his location. I later learned, sadly, that this first wild release was not successful—the young adult male died about a year after he left the enclosed part of the reserve, probably mauled in a fight with a more established wild male.

Even more tragically, the reserve at Wolong was badly damaged by the 2008 Wenchuan earthquake. Several reserve employees died, as did one of the captive pandas, crushed when a wall of her masonry cage collapsed. The degree of damage, plus the elimination of many surrounding bamboo groves, made it impossible for the reserve to be reestablished quickly.

Many surviving pandas and staff were temporarily relocated to the Bifengxia Panda Reserve, near the small city of Ya'an. During the academic year 2008-2009, when I taught nearby at an agricultural university, I had several chances to see the Bifengxia pandas. On my final visit, in spring 2009, I showed two American friends around. Through a plate glass window, we viewed one of the park employees feeding a baby panda a supplemental bottle. We followed twisting paths past the juveniles' play yards, the large enclosures for adult pandas, and the quarantine areas for pandas about to be shipped to zoos in other parts of the world. The acreage of the center was only about a hundredth as large as Wolong, but there was plenty of space for a captive breeding program and nurture center.

"Wow!" my friend Kim remarked. "Zoo panda exhibits will never be quite the same after our experiences here."

We saw almost 60 pandas in all, along with signage in both Chinese and English explaining some of the pandas' behavior. Several of the bamboo species that pandas prefer were being cultivated in hillside tracts. Breeders and veterinarians had also come up with dietary supplement blocks containing apples and carrots, fortified with other important nutrients. Pandas ate these along with their favorite forage— lots and lots of bamboo, harvested and placed into their enclosures several times each day.

A second chance to see wilder areas of China came during the school year 2006-2007, when I was teaching far inland at the edge of a huge desert. As the weather chilled, I again asked for my colleagues' advice:

"Is there someplace warm, sunny, humid, and breezy where I can get away from the Xinjiang weather during winter break?"

Several of my more widely traveled teaching colleagues recommended Sanya, a former fishing village on Hainan Island, dubbed the "Hawaii of China." As I shivered through a bleak December, their suggestions fell on willing ears. With their help, I booked airline tickets and made hotel reservations. Once fall term classes were over, I headed south. During my four-week Hainan holiday, I found parts of Hainan Island in the South China Sea to be a tropical paradise, just as advertised. Cascades of bougainvillea, most often in vibrant shades of pink, red, and purple, bloomed in profusion along the coast. One of our guides told us that twenty different varieties of the trailing shrub grew in the area.

A local connection gave us chances to get beyond some of the tourist kitsch that too often clutters scenic wonders everywhere. I had an opportunity to visit a natural area of curving white sand beach at Yalong Bay, its wide arc and the graceful rolling waves beyond screened by tropical foliage from the upscale tourist complexes that lined part of the coast. I went on a circle tour of the island via a recently completed nearshore expressway. Settled areas alternated with stretches of coastline that looked untouched by human activity. One day a Chinese friend escorted me to a hilltop nature preserve several miles inland.

"These are the lungs of Hainan," he said. "If we destroy this tropical forest, much of the lushness and the clear waters that make our resorts possible will be destroyed with it."

My third chance to visit a unique landscape in China came courtesy of my more media-savvy husband. Without his nudging, I wouldn't even have been aware of the natural area we visited most recently. Jim was entranced by the movie "Avatar." After seeing it several times, he set out to find out what had inspired the magnificent scenery of the film. He learned that many of the landscapes in the film had been adapted from China's very first National Forest Park, established in 1982 in a remote area of Hunan Province subsequently renamed Zhangjiajie. Still somewhat hard to get to without benefit of a group tour, Zhangjiajie was nevertheless at the top of Jim's "must-see" list when we started planning an extended trip to China for late spring of 2017. Whenever practical in China, we prefer land travel to air—that way we see more of the countryside and have more chances to interact with average Chinese. However, when we did internet research before leaving the U.S., we couldn't find any direct trains or buses to Zhangjiajie from any of our previous stops.

We hoped to get advice and assistance from Chinese friends living in cities we planned to visit earlier in our trip. We figured that once we got to Zhangjiajue, we'd be able to stay in a hotel in town, then figure out a way to get to the park itself by walking or bus or taxi. I brought up a few internet pictures of the park to see what had thrilled Jim so much. Full of stone spires and towers, it looked vaguely like Zion National Park in the U.S. Southwest, but with trees and other sub-tropical vegetation. I doubted I'd enjoy the place as much as Jim did—I'm not a big sci-fi fan and hadn't liked Avatar all that much, but I figured it would be worth a detour to help preserve family harmony.

With overnight hotel stays in between, it took us three separate train trips, mostly along stretches of the Yangtze River, to get from Chengdu to the smallish city of Zhangjiajie, the gateway to the park. A Chengdu-based friend helped us make hotel reservations and buy train tickets first through the mammoth Yangtze River city of Chongqing, then to smaller Yichang, and finally to the park's entrance city. The evening our train arrived at Zhangjiajie was misty and smoggy. A near-constant drone of airplanes in a landing pattern made conversation difficult. No one at the tourist information center spoke English or seemed to understand my Mandarin attempts to locate the hotel where we'd booked a room.

I sulked. All this way to see a crummy park in the middle of nowhere? Why hadn't we come by plane, just this once? Where the heck was our hotel? After several false starts, we located the hotel, more like a hostel, really, a couple of blocks away. Well after midnight, the drunken party going on beneath our window finally subsided. The following morning, I was awakened at dawn by sounds of a plane, a garbage truck, and a rooster, in that order. This park had better be worth it! Once we straggled down to the hostel's reception desk, our luck improved. Our innkeeper was fairly fluent in English and had a good stock of multilingual maps of the area with descriptions of the park's major attractions.

"Go across street to local bus station," she said, while scribbling on a card. "Show this card to people there. They direct you to right bus to go to park. Cost 20 yuan each way (about three dollars). Once you finish day's touring, get same bus line back to town."

After we'd jounced around for about half an hour on the bus, the weather cleared a little as we neared the park. The air got less polluted, too. Foreigners like us were ineligible for a senior discount, so we paid the full entrance fee—the equivalent of about $40 U.S. for each of us. As I continued to grumble, Jim reminded me that these park passes were good for four days, and we would most likely make full use of them. We followed other pedestrians from the park's entrance to a park bus that took us in turn to the entrance to a cable car. For an additional 22 dollars each, we were lifted through the mists to the top of the park.

As we walked trails and spent time at successive overlooks, I finally began to understand what had motivated Jim. This really was a unique environment. The overlooks nearest the cable car station were crowded in late May, but enough trails branched off in different directions so that it was possible to wander relatively undisturbed around much of this upland area. The trail network threaded its way through areas not yet eroded into sandstone pillars and crags thousands of feet high. Ranges and ranges of them stretched far into the mists in fanciful formations in front of us. As we descended one stretch of trail, I heard rustling in nearby trees.

"Look," I whispered to Jim, "monkeys!" A small troupe were swinging from branch to branch along the edges of a burbling creek. A couple of them descended to ground level to drink from a pool where the stream temporarily slowed.

Earlier, a Chinese friend had warned me about aggressive monkeys at a different mountain park. I held tight to my day pack. At later rest stops, I noticed with relief that these monkeys did not beg or approach humans closely. However, they didn't hesitate to raid local trash bins for any leftover tidbits.

Our first day in the park we spent mostly at its upper level. On later days, we partly explored other upland sections close to a glassed-in elevator near a different park entrance. We also took the chance to follow the Golden Whip River from one park entrance to another—about five miles. Lined with sand-colored rocks, Golden Whip was a clear stream that rippled its way through the lower reaches of the park. A riverside trail was laid out with frequent vistas looking up at some of the closer crags. None of our pictures could do the landscape justice. If I ever watch Avatar again, I won't bother much about the plot. I'll instead be paying close attention to the landscapes that inspired the Hallelujah Mountains.

Prior to 2004, my visits in China had provided limited chances to experience China's natural areas. In 1980, though our tour group did spend time in the countryside, everywhere we went we encountered a landscape repeatedly sculpted and rearranged by humans. The non-tourist-guide Chinese I encountered then were still too busy with basic necessities to be much interested in far-flung travel or much concerned about the natural environment. The majority of factory workers put in six shifts each week. Days off were staggered so that industrial plants could run non-stop. There was no such thing as a weekend. If the weather was pleasant, groups of workers from the same factory or work unit might visit a nearby urban park together on their one day off— anything further afield was hard to imagine. Back then, too, the country's over 600 million peasant farmers made up four-fifths of the population. Like small-scale farmers everywhere, they rarely got any days off, except in northern areas in the depths of winter.

As China's booming economy lifted hundreds of millions out of poverty, both government agencies and the increasing number of private companies reduced weekly work hours to include more holidays and vacations. Internal tourism began to thrive. Transportation infrastructure via road, ferry, high-speed rail, subway, or air travel improved by leaps and bounds. By the early 2000s, many middle-class Chinese owned private motorcycles or cars. Chinese with newly available discretionary income longed to see places of natural beauty. Nearly every middle-class Chinese urbanite had a dream vacation spot, either in-country or overseas. The increasing in-country tourism infrastructure in China made it possible for me too to see regions that had previously been off-limits or just too hard to get to.

A couple of years after my 2004 teaching and travel, my first long-term China adventure would provide chances to explore hard-to-get-to areas that encompassed some of China's climate and ecological extremes, along with some of its most strenuous efforts to tame them.

9

Iron Rooster Redux: by Train into the Desert

明月出天山。

I don't deny that traveling in China is exasperating, or that China has political, social and economic problems. It is a poor, totalitarian country whose people are in a state of confusion: Are they Marxist? Are they Maoist? Are they democratic? What does "democratic" really mean? What is worth salvaging from their traditional past?

Paul Theroux, *Riding the Iron Rooster,* 1983.

One evening in early August 2006, my husband Jim and I left a comfortable tourist hotel in the Chinese city of Xi'an and boarded an overnight westbound train. For much of its long history, Xi'an has served as a pivot point between China's more settled eastern regions and its "Wild West." Jim and I were partway through an extended train journey across much of northern China toward our first full-year assignment as foreign English teachers, in the small town of Ala'er, Xinjiang. We would travel next to Jaiyuguan, the western terminus of China's Great Wall. My subsequent adventures in Jaiyuguan and elsewhere would reinforce two opinions I'd developed in earlier travels in China:

•Traveling without a bilingual tour guide in non-tourist China would tax my still-limited language and cultural skills.
• Fate often made allowances for a well-intentioned bumbler.

We'd been able to get from our initial arrival city of Beijing as far as Xi'an with the assistance of English-speaking Chinese friends and helpful travel agents, but the further we got from Beijing, the fewer local people we knew and the less likely we were to encounter English-capable travel agents. Once we arrived in Jaiyuguan, we knew no one. We had met no fellow passengers we could ask for help. We got ourselves and our luggage off the train. Then I approached the station clerk to buy tickets for the next stage of our westward journey. This was the first time I'd tried to buy train tickets directly, rather than having a friend or travel agent purchase them for me.

The clerk did not at first understand my halting Chinese, so I pointed at appropriate words and phrases in my now-somewhat-tattered Mandarin phrase book:

"Two tickets. One-way. Tonight. Urumqi (the capital city of the next region west)."

"*Mei you*" (pronounced like the abbreviated version of mayonnaise), she said, shaking her head from side to side. Roughly translatable as "don't have," *mei you* has become one of my least favorite Chinese expressions.

How about tickets for the following day? Same response. Day after tomorrow? Still *mei you*. More attempts for different days yielded the same result. Temporarily stymied, I suggested to Jim we find a hotel in town. We hadn't slept well on the train the previous night and a hotel respite with clean sheets and private bath would be a good interlude before resuming our trip.

Some backstory: by late 2005, Jim and I were hard pressed to keep up with speedily occurring changes in computer software technology. We were no longer on the cutting edge. Increasingly, we were billing our clients for babysitting creaky older systems that would eventually be replaced. Though we likely could have continued to earn a comfortable, if boring, living doing software maintenance for several more years, we hoped for something different. Slightly seasoned after our earlier short-term teaching assignments in China, we leaned toward an experiment with longer-term teaching and travel. While searching the internet for possibilities, Jim came across a help wanted listing for foreign English teachers in Ala'er, Xinjiang, China, at Tarim University. Where the heck was that?

We found enough English-language description to learn that the college had been founded as a "desert reclamation school" during the 1950s, shortly after the advent of the People's Republic of China. Its primary aim at first was to train agricultural agents in techniques for taming and irrigating this area over twice the size of France, with fertile soil but very limited water, few settlers, and sometimes hostile neighbors.

The school was in northwestern China, near borders with what had earlier been Soviet republics and were now Kazakhstan, Kyrgyzstan, and Tajikistan. A narrow strip across one mountain pass led to Afghanistan. Via internet, we also learned that Ala'er was a small oasis town on the Tarim River in the northern part of the Taklimakan Desert, Asia's largest.

This part of China is officially not a province but an "autonomous region," one of several with substantial non-Han ethnic populations. Xinjiang's main group are the Uyghurs (pronounced "WEE-grrrrz," with lots of variant spellings), nomadic pastoralists most of whom practice Islam. The Tarim River, whose watershed supports much of the area's population, is formed by the juncture of several glacier-fed streams flowing out of the mountain ranges that surround the bowl-shaped Tarim basin. The river provides irrigation and household water for about ten million people before it dries up a thousand miles further east.

If we went to Ala'er to teach, we would be much closer geographically and culturally to Kazakhstan's capital city than to Beijing. Teaching at Tarim University sounded like an adventure. The region's general lack of medical infrastructure could become a bigger issue as we aged, so if we went, we'd be wise to have our Xinjiang adventure sooner rather than later.

For several months in early 2006, Jim negotiated employment arrangements via email. Once we'd settled on a contract, we got our official invitations from the school, which we used to get the "class Z" visas that would allow us to work in China. After our assignments were secured, we sold our house and most of our belongings, stored minimal household goods with relatives, and packed for a long trip. Before heading across the Pacific, we took a circuitous route across much of the U.S. and Canada, visiting with friends and relatives along the way. We wound up in San Francisco in late July 2006, shipped a few essentials ahead to a Chinese friend in Beijing, then boarded a plane for the Chinese capital.

Once we arrived in Beijing, we at first weren't sure how we would use the roughly four weeks before our contracted late August appearance at school. Several days in the Chinese capital gave us time to adjust to the new time zone and reunite with old friends. Their input, plus our sense of adventure, helped us decide to go to Ala'er in stages, mostly by train. We'd stop multiple times to explore cities and towns along the way. Most Chinese still traveled by train then, especially in China's less-developed west.

We didn't set a fixed itinerary, preferring to adjust our travel plans as we went along. A Beijing friend helped arrange the purchase of train tickets for our journey's first leg. We'd head to Zhengzhou, the capital of Henan province, where we'd taught briefly in 2002. After a couple of days there, facilitated by the vice principal of our former school, we caught another day train to Xi'an and spent several days touring its area. We visited the famous terra cotta army, walked along sections of the restored city wall, saw the city center's bell tower and wild goose pavilion. I found a hotel travel agent who got us train tickets onward to Jaiyuguan--my first overnight Chinese train trip since 1980.

Here in Jaiyuguan, Jim hailed one of several taxis parked outside. Through sign language and a crudely drawn diagram of a large building with three stars, Jim got the taxi driver to deposit us at a tourist hotel near the town center, about a ten-minute ride from the train station.

China in 2006 used a five-star system to rate rentable lodging. A single star meant a hovel, something barely habitable, with minimal cleanliness and facilities. Two stars represented a basic room, sometimes with a communal bathroom at the end of the hall. Three stars was the minimum for lodgings officially open to foreigners: private bath, clean sheets, clean room, if sometimes a bit small. Four-star and five-star hotels represented increasing levels of luxury and expense. We'd stayed in such places earlier, but at this juncture we were in the middle of nowhere and had no idea how long it would be before we received our first paycheck. Avoiding excess spending on luxurious accommodations seemed prudent.

We settled into our room and checked the mattress on the double bed. It proved less than board-hard, but adequately firm and long enough, barely, to fit Jim's six-foot frame. Then we looked into the bathroom, whose fixtures were sparklingly clean, with a sit toilet plus enclosed shower stall. We unpacked a little and discussed what to do next. The hotel was conveniently located next to a park, with restaurants and some small shops nearby. Since we appeared stuck in Jaiyuguan for a while, we decided to do as much local sightseeing as we could while we tried to figure out how to get further west by train.

After restorative naps and showers, we headed across a traffic circle to the park. A short distance in, we found a bench to watch a fountain send spray into the late afternoon sunshine. A Chinese flute melody played softly through surrounding speakers. The fountain spouted elaborate patterns of high and lower jets, straight and swirling water, much like some I'd once seen along the Las Vegas strip. Young children ran between the water jets or splashed in the fleeting puddles on the metal grids at the fountain's base. After about five minutes, the fountain and speakers abruptly shut off. The children headed toward some other playground equipment, shepherded by gray-haired adults we guessed were their grandparents.

In a shady area, I noticed a group of metal riding toys—first a pig and a rooster—then the entire set of twelve figures, child-sized symbols of the Chinese zodiac: rat, ox, tiger, rabbit, dragon, snake, horse, goat, monkey, rooster, dog, and pig, each figure representing a different lunar year. Their backs were worn smooth and shiny from contact with lots of young bottoms.

I managed a phrase-book-assisted dinner at a local restaurant without any dire digestive consequences. I slept well. The following morning, Jim hailed a taxi. We wanted to go to the area's main tourist attraction, the restored fort at a pass, "The First and Greatest Pass under Heaven," about five miles away.

"*Duoxiao qian?*" I asked the woman driver (meaning "How much?" and pronounced roughly "dwah-shah-ow chen"). I pointed to the fort's location on a bilingual city tourist map Jim had found in the hotel lobby the evening before.

"*Yi bai quai,*" (yee ba-yee kwa-yee,) she responded. (One hundred Chinese RMB, or roughly $13 at 2006 exchange rates.)

After a quick conference with Jim about fare and arrangements and unable to remember how to ask "one way or round trip?" I resorted to my tattered phrase book. Via a combination of phrase book, map, and gestures, I negotiated that the driver would take us, wait, and bring us back to our hotel for the quoted price. A bargain, it seemed to me. We got in.

The fort was west of town, straddling the narrowest portion of a corridor between two high hills. Our map's commentary explained that the fort had been built to guard against barbarian invaders who could descend toward China through the pass. I'd learned earlier of a long-held Chinese dynastic tradition regarding dissidents and criminals. For most of a millennium, officials who had greatly displeased the emperor were summarily executed, along with their immediate and extended families. Those whose transgressions were less severe were only expelled beyond the pass, making this fort their last view of civilized China before being consigned to the wilds of the barbarian-infested northwest.

Much of the fort had recently been reconstructed. It was tall, square, thick, appropriately forbidding, with concentric sets of walls and gates to keep invaders out and soldiers in. It had its own water supply. A holding pond to one side supported a luxuriant growth of shoreline willows. The fort's parapets towered many feet above the surrounding ground. Various sections of the fortress held barracks or kitchens. At the center was a large open courtyard. To the east, parts of the Great Wall stretched into the distance, sometimes little more than crumbling piles of packed earth. To the west was a landscape of bare earth and rocky outcrops, with very little vegetation. A few camel drovers had tethered their animals within westward sight of the fort, hoping to entice tourists into paying for a ride. Satisfied that we'd seen most of the fort's features, we returned to our taxi and town.

Once back at our hotel, we started our final Jaiyuguan adventure—how to leave? Toward the end of the afternoon, I located a hotel employee who spoke some English.

"We want to go to Urumqi by train, but cannot buy train tickets," I explained.

"No problem," she responded. "I have friend who buys tickets. Good travel agent. You go to train station tonight at 7. He meet you there. Give him this card."

As I'd learned through experience, most long-haul Chinese passenger trains have four categories of accommodations, in ascending order of comfort and expense: hard seat, soft seat, hard sleeper, and finally soft sleeper, an accommodation I'd been treated to during my initial

China group tour back in 1980. Soft sleeper tickets cost nearly as much as a comparable airline flight and are often difficult to obtain. Here in Jaiyuguan, hard sleeper tickets would probably have to do.

Before we could board the train, we needed to taxi to the train station, which we managed just before 7. Then we had to find our contact. At long last he approached us, the only foreigners around. He was trailed by a group of drunken young Chinese men who also wanted hard sleeper tickets on the next westbound train. Their slurred Chinese made up in volume what it lacked in distinctness.

Minutes before the train left, about half an hour behind schedule, our travel agent presented the required quantity of tickets first to us, then to the merry younger Chinese. We grudgingly but gratefully paid, took our tickets, checked for the car number printed on them, then hoisted ourselves and our luggage onto the lengthy overnight train. After they'd paid in turn, the drunken young men headed for a different part of the train, and we never saw them again. A kindly train conductor helped Jim and me locate the appropriate car and berths.

Our compartment had six metal bunks, three to a side, each with a flimsy mattress, a bottom sheet, a quilt, and a pillow. A doorway opened onto a window-lined corridor that ran along one side of the train. The window at the other side of the compartment held a curtain that could be pulled shut to reduce light from outdoors when needed.

Metal ladders fixed to one end of each set of bunks provided access to the higher bunks and to overhead storage space. Every bunk had a small light and a small wall-mounted mesh container. We would occupy the two bottom bunks, more convenient to get in and out of, especially in the middle of the night. At one end of our train car was a wash basin, a squat toilet enclosure, and a large urn of boiled drinking water.

Once we'd settled in, we made some very basic Chinese conversation with our compartment-mates, a polite quartet of geological engineers on a short educational tour. We invited them down from their upper berths to share seats on our bunks until lights out.

After climbing down and joining us, the engineers pulled out a couple of carry-out containers. The senior engineer inquired, "*Nimen chi fan le ma?*" (pronounced roughly "nee-mun chuh fan le ma," meaning "Have you eaten?"). To assist us in understanding, he moved his paper tray of spicy-looking food toward us. In earlier travels, we'd sometimes been greeted with this expression rather than the "How are you?" that Americans more typically expect. Maybe another holdover from famine times? Jim ate a bit more than I did, both of us using pairs of disposable chopsticks that our neighbor also offered.

In a mixture of sign language, Chinese, tourist brochure, and fractured English, our compartment-mates enthusiastically recommended that we change our itinerary to stop off and visit a set of Buddhist caves, their destination.

"We leave train at twelve (midnight)," the head engineer pointed to his watch. "Then take taxi to Dunhuang. Tomorrow we see cave paintings. Very famous. Very beautiful. You come, too?"

Too spooked by my earlier misadventures to brave this midnight detour, I did not accept their advice. After the engineers left, Jim and I hunkered down in our now-private compartment and slept until early morning. Once the sun rose, I took one of the pull-down seats in the corridor and gazed out the window. Much of the surrounding land was desolate, but there were also stretches of green pasture, irrigated farm fields, even orchards in places. Intermittently, pomegranate trees lined the tracks, their bright red fruits a welcome contrast to the generally gray-brown surroundings.

About mid-morning, we stumbled off the train in Urumqi to a cacophony of taxi horns, shopkeepers' cries, and sometimes discordant music. We found a taxi driver who agreed to take us to the closest large three-star hotel, where I thought we'd easily find a room in this isolated inland city. On arrival, the driver took payment, gave us a receipt, deposited us and our luggage at the front entrance, and promptly left. At the reception desk, I inquired in halting Mandarin about room rates. They were very sorry—all their rooms were already booked. Was there a different hotel nearby with available rooms?

"*Mei you*," the expression I had come to dread.

I wanted to curl up into a fetal position and sob, right there in the hotel lobby. It turned out that most area hotels were full in August. Urumqi was crammed with Chinese travelers from further east, spending their summer holidays in the dry, less smoggy desert air.

Then I heard the cadences of English nearby—as it happened, a visiting American professor from Montana and his bilingual translator. Incredibly, the translator was able to connect me by phone with the only person Jim or I knew who had even the remotest connection with Urumqi: the young former travel-mate who'd provided translation assistance for us during our 2004 China Youth Travel tour in Sichuan. Then, we'd given him the English nickname "Urumqi Frank" because of his birthplace and his open demeanor. We didn't know much about him, only that when we first met him he'd nearly finished university at a prestigious college in Sichuan and was traveling as a sort of pre-graduation present. Now he was back in his hometown. Unlikely as it seemed for an ambitious recent college graduate from a top Chinese university further east, Frank was again living in Urumqi.

Frank met us at that first, fully booked hotel and took us by taxi to his family's apartment, a spacious two-bedroom walk-up on the fourth floor of an extensive mid-rise complex built for railway workers during the 1970s. As soon as we walked into the apartment, we saw evidence of recent, hasty cleaning and straightening. On the floor in one corner of the living room were six medium-size watermelons.

"Please, sit," Frank motioned us to cleared spaces on the sofa along one wall. "Would you like some watermelon? They're in season at the local markets, so I bought several."

He found some paper plates, and gave each of us a slice of the deliciously sweet, juicy melon. A little later, he offered us free lodging on the apartment sofa for the rest of our Urumqi stay.

Jim and I exchanged glances.

"Thanks very much for the offer," Jim told him. "It's wonderfully generous of you. However, we're not great at adjusting to Chinese squat toilets. Do you think there are any hotel rooms for foreigners available not too far away?"

Frank went to work almost immediately. He phoned a high school chum who soon joined us. The two spent an hour working their cell phones and computers in tandem. Success! They found us a room for three nights at a three-star hotel on a side street nearby. They then took us out for a celebratory lunch at a local Uyghur restaurant.

Uyghurs predominated in this region before recent decades' immigration from majority-Han areas had diluted their influence. As most Uyghurs are Moslems and follow Islam's dietary practices, they do not eat pork. Protein at Uyghur restaurants is mainly mutton, very tender, delicious mutton. We stuffed ourselves with kebabs, noodles, and a hearty stew. After lunch, Frank called a taxi to deposit us at our next hotel, promising to phone in the morning.

Frank's hospitality was wonderful, but with the crowded conditions in Urumqi's hotels, we knew we'd need to move on, perhaps as early as three days from now. We'd need to book train tickets to get further west. When Frank called, we asked if he could show us how to get tickets for the rest of our train journey. Frank said he was busy that morning, but would meet us again for lunch. He'd explain then how to buy tickets for Chinese trains.

"Buying tickets at a train station is not the normal way," he began. "You get them either in hotels, at banks, or at special travel agencies, several days or weeks before your trip. You can only buy tickets leaving from your current city. Journeys with more than one step have to be booked in separate stages. Trains fill fast this time of year. Students return to universities; families return home from vacations. Later, I'll help you get tickets."

Over further lunch conversation, we learned more about Frank's background. His well-educated parents had been exiled to Xinjiang during the Cultural Revolution under suspicion of being too friendly to outsiders—a cousin had studied briefly in a Western country. When Frank was a teenager, his father had abandoned his mother for a younger woman. Frank rarely saw him anymore. Frank had come back to Urumqi only a few weeks earlier—he'd learned that his mother was seriously ill. Though he'd originally had other plans, he'd dropped everything else to hurry home. As an only child, Frank felt a special responsibility toward his mom, who was undergoing in-patient breast cancer treatment at a specialized area hospital. Frank visited her every morning.

"I'm so sorry," I said. "What an awful ordeal, for your mom and for you. It's wonderful of you to have helped us, with everything else that's going on. I feel bad we've imposed on you like this."

"Not a bother, really," Frank answered. "Actually, being able to help you find your way around has taken my mind off Mom's troubles for a while."

After a few more bites, I re-entered the conversation.

"I don't often talk about it," I told Frank, "but I was diagnosed with breast cancer about nine years ago. It seems an odd coincidence that I'm here sharing lunch with you while your mom is dealing with the same challenge. I've never met your mother, but I feel connected by our illnesses somehow. If she's feeling up to it, do you think she'd be willing to have me visit, to show that it's possible to live a full life after breast cancer treatments are over?"

"I'm not sure," Frank responded. "She has good days and bad days. How about I phone her tonight and then let you know at your hotel?"

He phoned our hotel room just before we settled for the night. His mom was getting stronger after her most recent treatment and would welcome me at the hospital. Could I come the following morning? I agreed, both eager to be of help and also curious about medical care in China. I'd never been inside a Chinese hospital or clinic.

As I dressed the next morning, I self-consciously dispensed with my bra and prosthesis, going bare-chested and lopsided under a loose-fitting shirt. Frank picked Jim and me up in a taxi that whisked us all to the cancer hospital, a modern-looking ten-story building on a main thoroughfare. Affiliated with a major university, this hospital provided cancer care for patients from throughout Xinjiang while training specialists to provide the best available modern treatments. As we all stepped into an elevator for the trip to Frank's mom's seventh floor room, Jim gave my hand a squeeze.

We entered a spacious, clean private room. It had less paraphernalia than I'd have expected in a corresponding American setting. The atmosphere seemed more relaxed and less germ-phobic. A window overlooked the broad avenue below. Frank's mom lay in an adjustable hospital bed; an additional cot was pushed against the far wall. Frank introduced us to his mom and to his mom's retired sister, who'd come to help with the caregiving.

"*Ni hao*," I stammered.

Frank's mom smiled despite the IV drip in her arm. Frank's aunt was busy washing grapes in a small sink. She soon came to join us.

"*Huanying* (welcome)," she said, and offered all of us grapes. I took some—another delicious specialty from parts of Xinjiang. While I savored the grapes, I related the basics of my own breast cancer scare. Frank switched nearly effortlessly between Chinese and English, seemingly unfazed by his dual role as son/translator.

"What medicines is your mom taking?" I asked.

Frank had trouble with some of the English medical terminology, but the names were similar in both languages. After a while, Frank and Jim went out into the hallway, leaving the women to ourselves. I'd been relieved to learn that his mom had undergone similar surgery and was doing follow-up treatments with some of the same chemotherapy drugs that had been used on me nearly a decade earlier. I smiled and gestured to accompany my limited Chinese vocabulary—a thumbs-up sign while showing my flat place and hoisting eight fingers.

"*Ba nian*," I stumbled out the Chinese expression for the years I'd been cancer-free. I smiled some more and hugged both mom and aunt.

Later that day, Frank and his hotel-room-finding sidekick took us to a bank branch where they knew some of the clerks. They got us hard sleeper train tickets to our terminal city of Aksu for the following Monday night, a few days after our current hotel reservations ran out. No problem, Frank said. He and his friend went back to their phones and computers and found us an alternate hotel for the gap days.

Our final train journey would get us to Aksu about a week earlier than we'd initially planned. Ever-helpful Frank got Jim email access to alert our school to the changed itinerary. We'd have to rely on the Tarim University staff to accommodate our revised arrival date. I was sad to be leaving Urumqi, but excited to be approaching our final destination.

The evening of our train, Frank and another friend, a burly fellow built like a football linebacker, hefted our luggage into a waiting taxi. Before we got on the train, we ate at a restaurant next door to the train station. The four of us shared a late supper of "big plate spicy chicken," a Xinjiang specialty. The dish consisted of large pieces of hacked bone-in chicken in a very salty sauce. Just after the waiter brought the dish to our table, he added a big portion of wide noodles on top of the meat and sauce. Frank and his friend ate their fill, then escorted us to the correct train, car, compartment, and berths, stowed our bags, and waved goodbye.

Eighteen hours later, we arrived mid-afternoon in the small city of Aksu, the closest train station to Ala'er and Tarim University. Since leaving Beijing, we'd crossed nearly 2,000 miles of China, seen cities, rivers, hills, farmland, forts, camels, greenery, and desolate scrub. We'd benefited from unexpected kindnesses. We'd coped with language difficulties, occasional sleep deprivation, and uncertain accommodations. If I'd found parts of the journey discouraging or scary, I'd never been bored.

Our luck held as we reached Aksu. The Foreign Affairs Officer from Tarim University, Mr. Mao, was on hand to meet our train, along with a school car and driver.

"Welcome to our university," Mao gushed in slightly accented English. "I hope you will be happy here in Xinjiang." Then he helped the driver stow our well-traveled duffels.

From Aksu, it was a jarring two-hour ride through the desert to Ala'er. Mao had arranged supper for us at the school's guest house, after which he led us to a spacious, sparsely furnished apartment on the fifth floor of a faculty housing complex near the eastern edge of campus.

It was 11 p.m. Beijing time. I was exhausted. Tomorrow would be soon enough to get a better idea of my future at this school, small by Chinese standards, with about 10,000 students. In the morning, I'd also begin to learn more about the surrounding small town (about 15,000 people) near the edge of a very large desert, over 1,500 miles from Beijing and over 2,000 miles from the nearest ocean. First priority, sleep.

10

Thanksgiving in the Desert

大漠沙如雪。

"The grassland is a big life, but it's thinner than people's eyelids. If you rupture its grassy surface, you blind it, and dust storms are more lethal than the white-hair blizzards. If the grassland dies, so will the cows and sheep and horses, as well as the wolves and the people, all the little lives."

Jiang Rong, *Wolf Totem*, 2004.

The Monday evening before American Thanksgiving, Jim and I sat huddled together on a black faux leather sofa in our first floor faculty apartment, sipping hot tea, talking about the upcoming holidays. When we'd first arrived in Ala'er in August, I'd been homesick. Sporadic emails over our maddeningly slow internet connection, plus an occasional static-laden phone call, were our most direct ways of staying in touch with family and friends back in the U.S. It seemed a very thin thread to home. As we got busy with classes and got to know some students and colleagues, my homesickness subsided. By October, I was reveling in the beautiful clear weather and the brilliant golden leaves of the oasis trees. I enjoyed excursions to see the Tarim River, the end of the cotton harvest, the irrigation canals sluicing through the desert, and the larger shopping possibilities in the railroad junction town of Aksu. However, as the holidays approached, my homesickness returned. I missed family, especially the son and daughter-in-law who'd sent word of a first grandchild to be born in the spring.

By early November the leaves had dropped. The weather turned abruptly colder. The university, following government standards, had activated its centrally controlled heating system. We had no choice about the level of warmth. Sometimes our apartment got so toasty we had to open the windows. At other times, temperatures indoors hovered just above freezing. Our apartment was roomy, but sparsely furnished. This pre-Thanksgiving Monday, our cavernous living quarters were chilly, despite our radiators' best efforts.

I'd decided to cope with my homesickness partly by creating an American-style Thanksgiving feast on the upcoming Saturday for some local students and colleagues. I mused about the menu, half talking to myself, half to Jim.

"The campus market has potatoes, sweet potatoes, onions, cabbage, beans, and carrots. On Wednesdays, the bake shop sells bread that's not too sweet. I can buy a couple of loaves to use in stuffing. I have some canned peas and canned corn I bought the last time I went to Aksu for shopping, plus some spices I brought from home. So the vegetables and stuffing are not a problem."

Then I paused, mentally ticking off meat options: local markets had chicken, either precut or alive, but Xinjiang hens were scrawny. It would take several birds to feed us. Early in the year I'd purchased a live bird and had it butchered—the available meat was barely enough for the two of us. I fretted that the meal just wouldn't be the same without its centerpiece bird. The closest available turkey, I thought, was likely to be at a large international grocery store in Urumqi, our region's capital city and its only large urban area. Billed as the "city furthest from any ocean," Urumqi was a 20-hour car-and-train ride back toward Beijing. Not sure if Jim was paying attention, I raised my voice slightly to be heard over the radiators' clanking.

"What *should* we do about a turkey?" I whined.

A few days earlier, I'd explained American Thanksgiving customs at "English Corner," a weekly evening English-language presentation Jim and I had set up where interested students, staff, and townspeople could come for English practice. The two of us alternated weeks, crafting programs about various aspects of English language and American life, with a question and answer period at the end of each session. For my most recent turn, I'd briefly told the story of the first Thanksgiving shared by the Massachusetts Pilgrims and local Indians in 1621.

"Settlers from England called Pilgrims came to America in 1620. They arrived at the beginning of winter. Their ships had gone north of their expected landing place. In the cold climate, many settlers died that winter. Even after spring came, the newcomers knew little about which crops to plant, how to hunt for meat, or how to build permanent shelters. Nearby Indians helped them a lot. After their first harvest, the settlers had a big celebration. They invited the local Indians and feasted together for nearly a week."

After I finished the Pilgrims' story, I went over the dishes typical of a modern American Thanksgiving meal. I even passed around a copy of a famous mid-twentieth century Norman Rockwell illustration: a plumpish grandmother making her grand entrance into the family dining room carrying a whole roast turkey, while the grandfather sat poised with carving knife and fork at the head of a large, heavily laden table. Other family members gazed on expectantly.

Among those attending my English Corner presentation were several of the younger Chinese teachers of English. They were very curious about this American festival and asked lots of questions.

The late evening chill deepened. We finished our tea. Jim provided no advice about the turkey problem. We were about to don our flannel pajamas, pile quilts on the bed, then try for a warm night's sleep, when we heard a knock at the door. We weren't expecting anyone. I looked through our peephole. Miss Zhang, a young English teacher, was standing on the stairwell landing with another young woman. They had put a large burlap sack on the floor between them.

Once I opened the door, Zhang launched into her carefully prepared English speech: "I imagine American Thanksgiving like you describe last week," she told me. "We want to help you celebrate, so we bring you a turkey."

I was temporarily speechless. Local colleagues and students had already been generous. Visitors to our apartment often brought fresh fruit, including delicious local pears, grown using irrigation water from the inland river that was the main reason for our town and university. Some of the other teachers had invited us to their apartments for simple dinners. Still, a turkey was a gift above and beyond.

Once my capacity for speech came back, I stuttered, "That's very kind of you. It must have been expensive. Please let me pay you." I wondered if I had enough cash to cover the price of a turkey.

"Oh, no," Miss Zhang protested, "No pay, please. Turkey not cost anything."

My curiosity was aroused. I wondered where she had managed to find a turkey in our small, isolated, oasis-in-the-desert town. Above all, how had she managed to obtain one for free?

She explained that her parents had an area small farm where they raised turkeys as brood hens—the hens' sitting surface was large; these "surrogate moms" didn't mind hatching out batches of chicks and ducklings in exchange for generous food allowances. Zhang's parents had willingly donated a hen to help the foreign teachers celebrate their American holiday.

I had little choice but to accept the gift. I thanked Miss Zhang. She handed me the sack, then cautioned as she turned to go:

"You should put in basement storage room. It smells bad."

Gingerly, I edged open the sack to view the bird. A spritely turkey hen cocked her head and peered back at me. Ten minutes before, I'd had no idea there were any turkeys within hundreds of miles. Now I was gazing at a live one.

By this point in our Ala'er stay, we'd learned to tiptoe around the tensions and distrust between some Han Chinese faculty and administrators and the Uyghur "minority" who made up parts of the faculty and a substantial portion of our school's student body. We'd decided to invite half a dozen Han friends, students and colleagues for our feast's main course, and to include several of our Uyghur students and friends in a larger group for dessert.

I enlisted fluently bilingual teacher and friend Jane Wang to help me get the turkey butchered, dressed, and refrigerated. With Jane's help, I also arranged to have the local grilled meat market slow roast the bird by halves on Friday, using their largest enclosed spit. Our town had no private ovens. Oven-based cooking was not an efficient use of expensive fuel, so only larger commercial enterprises had ovens. The spit was our best alternative. Teacher Wang also interceded with the local bake shop to give us the use of their commercial oven on Friday night after closing. We hoped it would still hold enough heat to bake apple and pumpkin pies for dessert. To round out the meal, I'd make stove top stuffing, basting it and making gravy with juices from an auxiliary chicken I could stew in our large wok. Just before the Saturday feast, I'd cook vegetables on our two-burner propane stove, then reheat some of the other dishes in our small Chinese model electric microwave-toaster-oven.

At the campus market, I discovered haw apples—bright red, small, round—a good local approximation of cranberries. Cored, heated, with added water, a little sugar, plus lemon juice for tartness, they made a pretty sauce.

On Friday evening, we thoroughly scrubbed our apartment. In the living room, we arranged our sofa, all our apartment's chairs, plus chairs loaned by our neighbors, into a rough circle. Just before our first guests were due on Saturday afternoon, I set the food out buffet-style on the counter in our narrow apartment kitchen, along with enough plates and utensils for everyone. Our feast consisted of turkey and stuffing, chicken, gravy, mashed potatoes, candied sweet potatoes, succotash, peas and carrots, sour cabbage, and haw apple sauce. Three pies—two apple and one pumpkin—plus a loaf of slightly soggy nut bread from our apartment "oven," constituted dessert. Absent any large tables, we would eat with plates on laps. Our best student, Andrew, insisted on tackling his turkey and stuffing, even the mashed potatoes, with chopsticks, while our other guests managed with forks, knives, spoons and fingers.

Our dinner guests compared our feast with Spring Festival, the biggest annual holiday for China's majority Han ethnic group. Both Thanksgiving and Spring Festival (or "Chinese New Year") emphasize extended family gatherings and sharing a generous meal.

"We always try to get home for Spring Festival," Andrew told us, "even if it takes several days on the train. It's often our only chance the whole year to visit with parents, grandparents, aunts, uncles, and cousins."

"Spring Festival has special foods, too, though we *never* eat turkey," kibitzed Jane Wang.

At dessert, some of the Uyghur students described the food customs of their most important festivals, two moveable Moslem feasts celebrated each year—one at the end of the holy month of Ramadan, the other about two months later.

"We have all kinds of treats," mentioned one pretty young woman student who generally dressed secular style, wearing sweaters and jeans and no head scarf. "Families get together and share delicious dishes the women have cooked ahead of time. Often the men have roasted a whole lamb, too."

It was well after dark before the final guests left. Jim and I took a little while to rest and unwind, then compared notes as we did the dishes and tidied the kitchen.

"Almost all the food is gone," Jim observed, "so we won't have to deal with leftovers. I'm glad everyone looked the other way when I dropped the drumstick I'd picked out for myself. At least the floor was clean."

"I noticed that the Uyghur students seemed most comfortable around Andrew," I remarked. "Maybe his efforts to get a 'Han/Uyghur Student Alliance' going are bearing fruit."

"Andrew is quite the big man on campus," Jim agreed. "He seems to have a hand in nearly every activity that goes on."

"I'm still a little homesick," I admitted, "but this was one of the most memorable Thanksgivings I've ever spent. So many people helped us prepare and celebrate. What a day!"

We dried dishes and utensils for a while longer, dividing the borrowed ones into piles to return to their respective owners the next day. The weather outside was still icy, but the apartment seemed much warmer than before. Once everything was as tidy as we could make it, we put on our flannel pajamas, piled quilts on the bed, and settled in for a good night's sleep.

When I'd arrived at Tarim University that August, worn out from our cross-country train journey, I hadn't been at all sure that the year would turn out well. That first night, I was too exhausted to notice how hard, short, and narrow our bed was by American standards. I got a decent night's sleep, anyway, then awoke to my first morning in a more or less permanent location. The world began to look more cheerful and inviting.

Our initial apartment was on the top floor of a 40-unit mid-rise building. Our front windows overlooked an athletic complex, with paved badminton courts, a track, basketball courts, and a few metal court-side bleachers. In the evenings, young guys often played pick-up basketball games, while girls or dating couples batted birdies back and forth across the badminton nets. Parents walked their toddlers around the edges of the track. At the back of our building was a rubble field in which both heavy equipment and workers with picks and shovels all engaged in moving materials around (a frequent condition all over China during the time I spent there).

We'd arrived about a week before the start of the fall semester. The school graciously housed us and helped us get settled before the bulk of the students arrived. We spent our pre-semester days learning where and how to shop, figuring out the basics of water, electricity, and internet access. All were intermittent, though our access to water improved after we requested and got a move to an apartment on a lower floor. We took walks around the campus and the surrounding town, sometimes accompanied by Foreign Affairs Officer Mao. Mao told us that the English translation of "Ala'er" was "jewel of the desert."

The part of town surrounding our campus had no stop lights, but was graced with many mature shade trees and a network of irrigation canals and drip lines. Some older members of the community still referred to Ala'er as "Town 9." They explained that the original names of settlements in this region had been derived from the regiment numbers of the People's Liberation Army soldiers assigned to patrol them. Gradually more civilian residents had moved in, but two of the three area high schools were still populated mostly with the children of locally posted soldiers. Most mornings, we were awakened by sounds of bugling, drumming, and marching coming from a drill field not far away.

As the first students began to trickle back to campus, we met a few of the bolder ones individually. Abdul, one of the students we met earliest, was a short, muscular Uyghur student majoring in tree protection. He rode all over campus on a bicycle. He wanted to practice his English with us. Abdul was proud of his Uyghur heritage, and resentful that official English classes were closed to him.

"The school will not allow us to take English," he complained. "Because much of our earlier schooling was in the Uyghur language, we have to take remedial Mandarin courses instead. My English is better than most of the Han students. I practice harder, too."

Over the course of our year in Ala'er, we would learn that Uyghurs made up just under 50 percent of the Xinjiang region's population, and about 40 percent of the student body at our school.

A couple of days later, Sheila greeted us while we were out on a campus evening stroll near the graduate student housing. She was a Han graduate student from Sichuan province majoring in plant science, one of a small group of about twenty graduate students among the much larger undergraduate population.

"Are you the new English teachers?" she asked in an accent that could have come from the Texas hill country in the U.S. where she has since settled. When we responded yes, she cracked a broad smile.

"Cool!" she said.

As we got to know her better, we learned that Sheila had spent several months during her high school years visiting in the United States. She had completed her undergraduate education in her native Sichuan. Then she'd opted for a graduate year in Xinjiang partly out of a sense of adventure. It was also a practical choice—the research project she wanted to conduct centered on one of the proteins in a plant similar to cotton that grows well in dry climates.

Then there was Andrew, an early-arriving sophomore who'd spent the previous summer with his aunt and uncle in Beijing. Nearly every day, he'd gone to a major tourist site, volunteering to provide free commentary to English-speaking visitors while improving his own language skills. Andrew's parents were natives of Inner Mongolia, in the north-central part of China. His father was a member of the Han Chinese majority; his mother was Mongolian. That autumn, Andrew placed first in the school's English-speaking contest. His intonation was flawless, though his accent was still recognizably Chinese. The content of his speech, bringing together themes of the richness of China's culture and the beauty of Mongolia's grasslands, was what most impressed the judges. Later in the year, Andrew introduced us to the English-language translation of a book that had become a Chinese bestseller: *Wolf Totem*, a novel set in the grasslands of his Mongolian homeland.

Getting started on our actual teaching took longer than we expected. The older campus building that housed the language learning classrooms was being refurbished and the project was behind schedule.

Foreign Affairs Officer Mao told us not to worry. We would be paid just as if we were working.

"Have a rest," he counseled.

It was something neither Jim nor I had anticipated. By the middle of the first week of regular classes, we'd gotten thoroughly bored. We begged Mao to let us meet with the chair of the English department and we suggested that the school might arrange for some part-time English lessons at alternate locations while we waited for the full-time classrooms to be ready. Mao, skeptical that anyone would request work beyond what was officially assigned, nevertheless agreed to arrange the meeting.

That is how we first met Jane Wang. Jane was not the head of the English department, but was a more recent college graduate than Amy, the department's forty-something leader. Jane was more comfortable with English. She accompanied Amy to the evening meeting and persuaded Amy to let us meet part-time with selected classes of students for the first few weeks until the language classrooms were finished. The following afternoon, Jane showed up at our apartment with copies of the language listening curriculum.

"Here are some of the teaching materials we use," she said, plopping them down on our smallish coffee table. "Most students are not very good at English," she elaborated, "but all must pass an English proficiency examination in order to graduate. We try hard to prepare them for this CET4 test. Since we are in a backward area, the passing score is lower than it would be in someplace like Beijing."

We chatted about her teaching experiences, her philosophy of education, and what had brought her to Xinjiang. Before I realized it, nearly an hour had passed and it was time to start dinner. We invited Jane to share in our rudimentary American-style meal: peanut butter and jelly sandwiches on local bread, with a glass of some powdered milk we'd brought with us from the U.S., then reconstituted using purified water. Jane surprised us by firmly insisting that she needed to return home to cook for her husband. Up until then, we hadn't realized she was married. She accepted one PB&J as take-out.

Jane is one of our favorites among the friends and acquaintances we've made over the course of our stays in China. Short and slender, with teeth angled oddly when we first knew her, Jane would qualify as a spitfire in any culture. She spoke a mile a minute in whatever language she happened to be using at the time—she knew some Japanese and French in addition to Chinese and English. Partly because of her teeth, partly because of her Sichuanese origins, Jane had an unusual accent in English. She had trouble with "n," "l" and "r" sounds, something more typical among Japanese speakers of English than among our other Chinese acquaintances. Jane struggled valiantly to make her accent more "native," all the while keeping a self-deprecating sense of humor about her "unique English." She confided that some of her less shy students had nicknamed her "Wang Wang," punning on her family name with the syllables used in Chinese for the barking sounds a dog makes.

Our formal teaching schedule puzzled us. Our primary function, we were told, was to model native speech for most first-year students. However, we were initially provided with pre-recorded language lab lessons alternating between British and American accents. Were we expected to speak at all?

Amy explained the seeming disconnect:

"Until recent years, Chinese teachers cannot travel outside China. It is hard even to go to Beijing or another big city. Most teachers keep their local accents. When they try to teach English, their pronunciation is very bad. Recorded lessons have standard pronunciation. That way, students can learn a proper way to speak. Teachers can still help with grammar and vocabulary."

Pretty quickly, we found relying solely on the recordings too limiting. We adapted the content and injected more interactive approaches. As Jane had warned, most of Tarim's collegians had limited mastery of English. There was little practical use for the language, since foreign tourists or international companies were rare in this part of Xinjiang. We gradually spent less time on class preparation and more time and effort coaching some of the Chinese teachers of English. Many of these teachers were quite young, only a few years out of university, and far away from their families further east. We were old enough to become their surrogate uncle and aunt. As time went on, we also spent more of our energy on extracurricular activities with the more interested students: weekly "English Corners," inexpensive restaurant meals, informal conversations during campus walks or visits at our apartment.

Mr. Mao arranged several outings for us during autumn's pleasant weather. The most memorable was an October weekend jaunt into the countryside surrounding the town. Mao knew a picnic spot with a large grove of variegated leaf poplar trees—a tree that can survive on the barest minimum of moisture. As the first frosts of autumn chill the desert nights, its leaves turn a brilliant yellow/gold. About a dozen members of the English faculty crammed into a school van and headed into the desert. After we'd spread our picnic on a blanket and eaten our fill, the younger men on the faculty began playing cards and challenging each other in a series of drinking games. Jim and I, plus the few women who'd been invited, crossed our fingers that someone would remain sober enough to drive us safely back to town.

By the middle of December, first term classes came to an end. We began the period when students embarked on two weeks of intense study and review before taking their end-of-term exams in their written courses. The other English teachers were busy preparing exams and compiling provisional term grades. Without classes to prepare or other teachers to socialize with, we were at loose ends. Christmas Day was not a school holiday—nearly the opposite. For most of the day, we sat around the apartment working crosswords, surfing the internet, and pacing our indoor spaces in search of something to do that did not involve bundling up and going out into the frigid weather for long periods. Then, mid-afternoon, the phone rang.

"Hello, Mr. Jim and Mrs. Jinny," said a vaguely familiar voice. "I would like to treat you to dinner with me at my favorite restaurant. May I meet you at your apartment at about six this evening?"

It took us a minute to register our caller's identity. Before we got off the phone, we'd confirmed that we were indeed talking with "Jesus," an older brother of one of the Uyghur university students. He ran an English tutoring business in town. Both the student, Iris, and her brother had been coming to our apartment on weekends all through the fall term to practice their language skills. So, on Christmas evening, we joined Jesus for a big plate spicy chicken supper at a local restaurant. The food was plentiful and tasty.

At the end of our meal, Jesus insisted on walking us back to our campus apartment. The night was clear, cold, and still. We'd nearly reached our building when we heard, coming over the campus loud-speakers, a rendition of "Silent Night," complete with English lyrics. For one brief moment, the juxtaposition of a Han-Chinese-administered university, a Moslem dinner host named Jesus, and a Western religious carol seemed the most natural thing in the world.

During our eleven months in Ala'er, we got recurring bouts of homesickness. We also suffered from recurring culture shock—Ala'er was very different from Richmond, Virginia, USA, even a lot different from Beijing. During our time on the Tarim University campus, we were the only Westerners in a radius of about 100 miles—Chinese friends told us there were a few foreigners in Aksu, but we never met them.

By December, the wind whipped around, making the outdoor cold seem even deeper. Indoor radiators were finicky, and buildings were rarely insulated. In January, as the semester came to a close, many students and staff had bad colds—real illnesses instead of just "exam flu." We also came down with something. By the time we fully recovered, we were more than ready for semester break—a chance for a change of scene, a possible reunion with Jim's initial houseguest Chen, and, best of all, warm weather. We would spend late January and early February along the shores of the South China Sea on the tropical island of Hainan, some of whose wonders I've described in the previous chapter. Once our month-long lunar new year vacation ended, it was time to get back to work.

The weather at last began to warm. The days grew longer. Siberian iris began poking up along the edges of campus walkways. Despite earlier warnings from Andrew and some of the veteran teachers, we were taken by surprise by the onset of dust storm season, a six to eight week springtime period of "yellow air." March winds in Xinjiang pick up dust from the Taklimakan Desert and blow it around, occasionally resulting in strong storms. The year we were there, we heard about a severe dust and wind storm that had derailed eleven train cars negotiating a mountain pass. Such storms stir up a ubiquitous haze that can last for weeks, until an infrequent rain comes through to settle the dust.

According to Beijing time (which was officially used throughout China, even in regions as far west as Xinjiang), the sun in late winter rose well after 9:00 a.m. It was typically 11 or even noon before sunlight pierced the haze enough to form shadows. The red disk then shone weakly for a few hours before disappearing back into the haze about 5 p.m. One March day just after lunch, while we were in our apartment preparing for afternoon classes, the school's alarm system sounded. The loud siren was followed by an announcement we couldn't understand. Mao soon phoned us with the English translation:

"Sandstorm getting worse. Afternoon classes canceled. Please stay indoors."

At the height of the storm, our efforts to take pictures out our apartment windows were fruitless. The camera's flash went off, but all that showed in the resulting photograph was a foot or so of murky brown air. We could barely see the willow trees lining the path outside our apartment block a few yards away. The storm abated nearly as quickly as it had come up. By sunset, the air, though somewhat dusty, had returned to stillness.

Almost before we knew it, we were engaging in farewell banquets and photo ops with students and colleagues. School officials, in a fit of generosity, underwrote a six-day end-of-contract trip for us and Jane Wang to other parts of Xinjiang before depositing us in Urumqi. We got to see the Flaming Mountains, to learn a little about the Uyghur "karez" irrigation system that had provided water to the low-lying oasis area around grape-growing Turfan for centuries. We finally rode on tourist camels. Near the petroleum-rich city of Korla, we had a picnic with an expatriate internet friend of Jim's. Jim and I, Jane, and several of Korla's other ex-pats sat on blankets and cushions in a grove beside the rapid-flowing Kongque River while local caterers prepared a lunch of kebabs, breads, and savory sauces. Afterwards, a few guys even went swimming, a special treat in water-short Xinjiang.

Before we'd left school, Mao had helped us book our flights from Urumqi back to the U.S., leaving a final free day for sightseeing in the regional capital. We bid goodbye to Jane at the train station, thanking her for being our colleague, guide and friend, holding out hope that our paths might cross again someday. The next morning, before heading for the airport, we visited the Xinjiang Uyghur Autonomous Region Museum. The main floor held impressive dioramas of the dwellings and customs of the many ethnic groups who make rural Xinjiang their home. Exploring further, we eventually found the exhibit we were searching for in the basement: a glass-encased mummy, the "sleeping beauty of Loulan."

Little is known about the life of this woman, who died at age 45 or so about 3,800 years ago. In death, her hair and features were preserved through a combination of desert dryness and the salt from the shallow lake area where she and others had been buried. She was Caucasian, a redhead. According to early DNA test results, she most likely came from an adjacent area of Siberia. Some of the burial artifacts found near her seem to indicate commerce and travel between other parts of Europe and Asia much earlier than previously thought—there are even pieces of cloth that resemble Scottish plaid. The notion that some of my long-ago Scots ancestors may have been to Xinjiang before me provided a comforting coda to this adventuresome year.

11

When The Earth Moved

地动山摇。

"Even though Yang Zhensheng has no memories of his own of the earthquake that flattened his hometown shortly before his birth, the disaster will forever be part of his life—he is named after it. In his given name, 'zhen' means earthquake and 'sheng' means birth. He was the first baby born in the rubble of Tangshan, a city that lies more than 150 kilometers (from) Beijing, after the 7.8-magnitude event which claimed more than 242,000 lives on July 28, 1976."

China Daily, July 27, 2016.

"Thanks for helping me walk Casey Dog," I told my grandson as we came in the front door of my older son's home in central North Carolina. Soon afterwards, I put the leash back on its hook and helped Peter and Casey settle into separate parts of the carpeted living room. Peter started playing with a set of blocks. Casey drifted off toward doggie dreamland. I went to the kitchen to get a glass of water.

I expected Monday, May 12, 2008, to be a relatively easy babysitting day—no after-school faculty meetings to extend our son's work day; nice weather so I could spend some time outdoors with toddler grandson Peter, my main reason for being in North Carolina.

My husband Jim and I had returned to the United States during the summer of 2007, despite other earlier plans. When we'd embarked on our first extended China teaching adventure, in August 2006, we'd expected to continue overseas English teaching for several successive years. Tarim University turned out not to be a perfect fit for us, but we were happy enough there to have welcomed a second year. After we'd been teaching for a couple of months, the school administration asked us to consider staying on.

We didn't give a yes or no response right away; instead, we asked for more time to consider our options. Both of us would turn sixty in the spring. Sixty was then the official retirement age for teachers in China. Our advancing ages might make getting future teaching assignments more uncertain. Being grandfathered in at a school where we were already teaching was our best chance for a continuing assignment. Though there were still exceptions, the retirement rule was becoming more widely and more vigorously enforced—China's educational system churned out over twenty million graduates at all levels each year. The new graduates needed jobs. Pensioning off older

Chinese workers was one way to open up opportunities for younger applicants.

We were still trying to decide what to do when we talked with our son and daughter-in-law in one of the weekend phone calls we pre-arranged a couple of times each month. They first confirmed the joyous news that we'd become grandparents the following spring. Then they hemmed and hawed a little.

Finally our teacher son explained, "Finding a good childcare situation for infants is harder than we expected. On days when Kerry works (as a nurse at a major hospital), she has twelve hour shifts. We haven't been able to find many childcare centers that open early enough for her to drop the baby off and still get to work on time. The few that do aren't located near us, and they have long waiting lists."

"We thought about trying to hire a live-in nanny," he continued, "but the expense is huge. We can handle the spring and summer of 2007 with Kerry's maternity leave and my summer vacation." He paused.

"Would you please consider coming to North Carolina to help us take care of the baby for the next school year? We'd be glad to help you find an apartment near our place."

Their request added another factor to consider. If we turned them down, we might not get another chance to be hands-on grandparents. We knew the upcoming first grandchild would be special. Getting to experience him or her as an infant could be a once-in-a-lifetime opportunity. The conversation brought back vivid memories of makeshift childcare arrangements and frantic mornings reshuffling work schedules when our own children were young.

I discussed my dilemma discreetly with a Chinese teaching colleague, June, who had a three-year-old daughter. Once June's daughter had been born, June's mother-in-law had relocated thousands of miles to Xinjiang to care for her granddaughter while June continued to teach at the university. June said that this arrangement was typical in China.

I'd read that in China's rural villages and more isolated areas, some Chinese grandparents even became full-time substitute parents while their adult children pursued more lucrative jobs in China's big cities. June teased me gently.

"You are becoming like a Chinese grandma," she told me.

At least for a school year, the grandparents in us won out over the teachers. I promised to do most of the day-to-day caregiving for 2007-2008 when our son and daughter-in-law needed assistance. Jim would help out occasionally.

Jim and I began readjusting to life in the United States. With help from our daughter-in-law, we'd found an apartment near our son's house, paid a deposit, and signed a year's lease. We furnished the place with the few belongings we'd stored before going overseas. Justin and Kerry pitched in with extras from their house. Starting in late August 2007, when our son's middle school teaching resumed, I walked the short distance from our apartment to our son's house two or three days each week. On babysitting days, I was the nanny from about 6:30 in the morning until our son returned in late afternoon from his job teaching math to eighth graders.

That Monday in May, I was temporarily without babysitting back-up, since Jim was away on a trip in China. Still, the school year was nearly over. I was coming down the home stretch. Peter was growing and developing fast. He had a few words, mostly in his own dialect. Whenever we went out in the yard, he was fascinated by the plants, bugs and rocks he found along the terraces and slopes at the back of the house. He loved to explore, then to show Grandma his treasures.

Mid-morning, the phone rang. Unusual. Our son and daughter-in-law were both at work. Their friends would know not to phone the house in the middle of the morning. Sometimes our daughter-in-law phoned just to touch base, but she typically timed her calls to coincide with her lunch break around noon. I thought the call might be from a telemarketer. I prepared for a brief, if annoying, conversation.

"Batterson residence," I said as I picked up the kitchen phone.

"I'm looking for Jinny Batterson," a pleasant but businesslike woman's voice said.

"This is she." Few people in this new town knew us, or even knew who we were. Who *was* this woman, and what did she want?

"I got your son's phone number from Hope Armstrong," she continued.

The wheels in my somewhat addled brain started spinning. Hope was the woman who had bought our previous house in the spring of 2006, when my husband and I had set off from Virginia to travel North America and then begin teaching English in China. Hope was both a gifted musician and an astute businesswoman—she was not likely to give someone our son's home phone number without good reasons.

The woman went on to identify herself, "I'm a human-interest reporter at the Richmond newspaper." A second or two of silence. "I'm looking for a personal account. Hope told me you might have a family member traveling in the earthquake zone."

"What earthquake?" On babysitting days, my morning routine rarely included time to listen to the news.

"There was a serious earthquake in Sichuan Province in southwest China about 2:30 in the afternoon their time. Hope said she thought your husband was traveling nearby. I wondered if you might have some insights based on his earthquake experiences."

Stop. Rewind. Take a deep breath. Get more information.

"Do you know what part of Sichuan?"

"The epicenter was near Wenchuan, a small city on one of the tributaries of the Yangtze."

As 2008 had turned from winter to spring, Jim and I were both missing China. If we could find a placement that would bend the rules a little to allow us to teach past the standard teachers' retirement age, we wanted to return there for the 2008-2009 school year.

In mid-April, Jim took off for a tourism/reconnoitering trip to China while I stayed back with Justin, Kerry, and Peter. Jim had a rough outline for a seven-week jaunt. He wanted to do a couple of weeks of vigorous mountain hiking with Jerry, an American friend about his age who would join him in China. Much of their itinerary radiated out from Sichuan's capital city, Chengdu. During the weeks before and after hikes with his friend, Jim would scope out possible Chinese teaching assignments for us as a couple for the following school year, either in Sichuan or the more southern regions of Guangxi and Yunnan.

The reporter's mention of the name "Wenchuan" triggered a recollection—Jim had also mentioned the town in an email he'd sent me a couple of days earlier. He and his American hiking partner had linked up with our Chinese friend and former student Sheila. They planned to drive north from Sheila's hometown of Dujiangyan in Sheila's small car, then do some day hikes in the Wenchuan area, staying in local inns overnight.

I briefly zoned out. Part of me stayed on the phone in a tract house kitchen near Raleigh, North Carolina, but a parallel Jinny started replaying mental images of a journey Jim and I had taken in 2004 through the same general area of Sichuan. After another deep breath, I was able to refocus on the telephone conversation. Earlier experiences of answering phones as a temporary office worker kicked in.

In my best customer-service voice, I managed: "My husband is in that area, but I don't expect further news from him for a few days—my guess is that he and his traveling companions are all right. May I get your contact information, please? I'll let you know as soon as I hear anything."

Once I got off the phone, I tried to stay as calm as possible so I wouldn't upset Peter. We made it through lunch without incident. He picked out a nap time story, I read to him, and then he drifted off to sleep. As soon as I was sure he wouldn't wake for a while, I brought up the internet on our son's computer. This is all the information I could glean at first:

At 2:28 p.m. local time on Monday, May 12, 2008, a massive earthquake first measured at 7.9 on the Richter scale shook Sichuan Province and surrounding areas in China's southwest. Shocks were felt as far away as northern Beijing and coastal Shanghai. Initial reports indicated no foreign casualties among the tens of thousands killed or missing, but transportation and communication systems were badly damaged. Definite reports were hard to come by.

The 2008 Sichuan earthquake impacted China in somewhat the same way as the 2001 World Trade Center terrorist attacks had the United States. People's basic assumptions about safety were shaken. This Chinese tragedy had a much larger nature-made component than the earlier American one, but both events also altered the sense of time of those affected: ever after, our lives are divided at the transition between our lives before and our lives after the tragedy.

Aftershocks from the primary quake would continue for weeks in this mountainous area with many swift-flowing rivers. Somewhere between four and eleven million people were left homeless. Bodies, cars, trucks, houses, even entire forty-six-passenger buses were buried beneath quake-generated landslides and may never be recovered. In the days following the initial tremor, "quake lakes" filled up in altered local terrain, threatening to add floods and drownings to previous damage.

I'd studied recent Chinese history enough to know that a similarly massive earthquake in northeastern China's coastal city of Tangshan in July 1976 had gone largely unreported. For a long time, very little news was released to sources outside China, and there was limited reporting even within the country. By some estimates, the Tangshan earthquake killed over 600,000 people. Centered about a hundred miles from Beijing, the quake damaged buildings as far away as the capital. Official records of the disaster released in 1988 by the Chinese Seismological Service listed 242,419 deaths. Whatever the actual human toll, this pre-dawn tremor in an area not previously known to be earthquake-prone was one of the deadliest natural disasters of the 20th century, yet much of the world knows little about this tragedy.

After that earthquake, offers of aid by other countries and international relief agencies were rebuffed. I wondered how China's leaders and citizens would react to this 2008 disaster. Would we ever learn for sure what happened and how many were killed? Of more immediate concern to me, would I ever be able to find out what had happened to my husband?

Communications technology had advanced by orders of magnitude during the thirty-some years between the two earthquakes, spurred in part by the reform and opening process leader Deng Xiaoping had initiated in the late 1970s. China's economy had boomed and seemed poised soon to become the world's largest. In May 2008, preparations were nearing completion for China's first ever chance to host the Olympic Games, to begin in Beijing on August 8, 2008.

Within hours of the initial shocks, Chinese Premier Wen Jiabao flew to the affected area to help assess damage and coordinate relief efforts. Relief supplies from Taiwan were flown to Sichuan's capital city

Chengdu soon after the quake. Within a few days, rescue teams from South Korea, Japan, Singapore, and Russia joined domestic rescue efforts. The International Red Cross sent supplies and rescue teams as well. In the weeks and months after the quake, condolences and relief supplies poured in from around the globe. The initial contrast with the reaction to the Tangshan earthquake was striking. Official casualty figures released in July 2008 listed 69,197 dead and 18,222 missing, with an additional 374,176 injured.

While Peter continued to nap, I did more internet research. I learned that the Wolong panda preserve, which Jim had mentioned as a sightseeing destination, was about 50 miles from the quake's epicenter. Because early reports indicated that much of the damage and loss of life had occurred in towns and cities when buildings collapsed, I was reassured. I reasoned that the hiking trio had probably been out of doors when the quake hit, with a good chance to escape with only minor injuries. When our son got home, I filled him in as best I could. Once back at our apartment that evening, I emailed out-of-town family and friends with the facts as I knew them. I asked for their prayers and kind thoughts. I comforted myself with images of Wolong's verdant pre-quake surroundings from our 2004 trip. My first night after learning of the quake, I slept fairly well.

The day after the earthquake was harder. Freed from babysitting chores by one of my daughter-in-law's days off, I worked from home on a part-time consulting assignment. I didn't get much done. As the hours crawled by, I compulsively tracked further media reports. Few reporters were able to reach anyone who had actually experienced the earthquake. My initial ignorance gradually morphed into agonized uncertainty. Well-meaning friends and relatives kept phoning and sending emails asking for more news. The coverage via television and internet showed more and more pictures of devastation—collapsed mountains as well as collapsed buildings.

I knew from our previous explorations near Wolong that the narrow river valleys of upland Sichuan are prone to landslides even without earthquakes. The evening of May 13, I went to bed early, but mostly tossed and turned. Finally I got up to check the internet again. It was well before dawn, but based on the 12-hour time difference with China, there might be news. After what seemed like an eternity to establish a connection, the internet came alive. There was a new email message, sent within the past hour or so:

"Dear Madam, Excuse please bad English. Husband and friends safe. Yours, Rick."

It would take several more months before I learned Rick was a close cousin of our friend Sheila. Sheila, Jim and I eventually reconstructed how Rick's message likely got through to me, via a combination of serendipity and far-ranging compassion:

Just after the initial quake, before cell phone coverage near Wenchuan was cut off, Sheila had sent a brief text message to her cousin Rick at his office in Dujiangyan's city administration. She told him she and her friends were unharmed.

For the first day or so after the quake, Rick had little time for anything except dealing with Dujiangyan's post-quake damage evaluation and helping other relatives and friends in that quake-stricken city. Still, he realized that Jim's and Jerry's families back in America would be worried about them. He began using short intervals between local rescue and removal efforts to try to find my contact information. He knew that Jim and Sheila had first met at Tarim University when Jim and I taught there in 2006. He was able to contact Mr. Mao, Tarim's Foreign Affairs Officer, to get my email address.

Some overseas communication lines that Rick had access to via his work survived the earthquake. He took time from his other duties to send me the brief message that meant so much.

It would be nearly another year before Jim and I had a chance to meet Rick in person and to thank him.

I am among the lucky families whose loved ones survived the earthquake with little damage. A day or so later, my husband was able to send his own email, confirming that he and his hiking partners were physically unharmed, though emotionally shaken. Jim flew back to the U.S. from Chengdu earlier than originally scheduled, since much of the remaining area he had planned to visit was inaccessible to all but residents and rescue teams.

It took a few weeks after he got home before we could discuss our respective earthquake experiences and impressions with each other in any depth. Jim had been panicked for a few minutes in the midst of the quake. He and his friends had been returning downhill after visiting a stone tower high above a small ethnic Qiang village when the earth began to shake. Soon, large boulders were jostled loose, tumbling down onto their path from higher up the steep hillside. For a short time that must have seemed like forever, Jim did a sort of jig.

"When the biggest boulders came loose, they made a pinging sound," he later told me. "I looked uphill toward them and tried to dodge them before they hit me. Smaller rocks came bouncing down, too. I was sure I was going to die."

Then, during a brief lull, Jim noticed that his two friends had taken shelter a hundred yards or so further downhill, under a large overhang of solid rock. He adjusted his dodging dance to move toward them and by the time the initial shaking stopped, all three of them were crowded into this semi-cave whose "roof" managed to hold.

The hikers were puzzled by what had happened. No one else was in their vicinity. The dust raised by the shaking earth made it hard to see very far. Their immediate concern was to reach a safer place. Figuring out what had occurred could wait until conditions settled down. They decided to continue downhill toward the nearest village. When they arrived, they found that some houses there had been damaged and that one car had been smashed by a boulder, but that no one had been killed or seriously hurt.

Just as they reached the edge of town and a wide spot in the trail, a small landslide came crashing down the hill and barely missed the village. Frequent aftershocks and landslides continued. Jim and his friends were happy to join the villagers. Village leaders began assessing damage and making plans for open-air shelters for the night, since no one would feel safe indoors. The sky was beginning to cloud over, promising rain by morning. One Qiang elder, noticing that the hikers were getting cold as the afternoon waned, risked injury or worse by going back to his stone and mortar house and extracting three warm full-length robes, which he gave to Jim, Jerry and Sheila to wear over their hiking shirts and shorts.

Still later in the afternoon, villagers arrived from a larger town further downhill that was accessible by paved road. Sheila had parked her car there before the day's hiking. These villagers insisted that the foreigners and their Chinese friend must retreat to their town, where they would be safer and better cared for. Jim, Jerry, and Sheila were not enthused. An excerpt from a narrative Jim emailed me from a hotel in Chengdu a week or so after the earthquake explained:

"We didn't want to move. The road we would have to use was right under an active landslide. After negotiating for a while, we gave in and made a run for it. We got through without incident, then assembled at a parking lot where Sheila's car was still sitting. We could see many houses caved in on the hillside above us. I heard no reports of fatalities in the town itself. Several had been killed while attending a hillside funeral nearby. The tower we had hiked to was no longer there. The people organized themselves to prepare food and shelter for the night. People whose houses had just been destroyed were making sure we were warm enough and had something to eat."

The following day, Sheila's car, having survived the earthquake, got towed behind a police vehicle at high speed over badly damaged roads to a still larger town, a district capital. District officials wanted to get non-relief-worker foreigners out of the quake area as quickly as possible. Jim, Jerry, and Sheila rode in the police cruiser, occasionally craning their necks to view Sheila's car careening along behind them on what remained of the road. By the time they arrived at the district town, Sheila's little Chery was just a twisted wreck, no longer drivable. Police interviewed the trio, getting Sheila to translate back and forth between Chinese and English. Officials arranged temporary housing for all three hikers at a local hotel. After a few more days, Jim, Jerry, Sheila, and several other foreign tourists who'd been in the vicinity, got caravanned the rest of the way back to Chengdu. So many roads in the quake zone were impassible that evacuation took them at first further west, then south, and eventually northeast to the capital. They were escorted by provincial authorities and rode in police vehicles.

In the small city of Ya'an, Sheila was met by her parents and her boyfriend, all overjoyed at seeing her safe and sound. Sheila's father sponsored an evening banquet at a local restaurant before the caravan made the remaining relatively short and smooth journey along the undamaged Cheng-Yan expressway. It was not until Jim and his companions got back to Chengdu that they became fully aware of the earthquake's scope.

By early summer 2008, Jim and I had reaffirmed our earlier decision to apply to return to China as a couple to teach English for the following school term. We soon were accepted for posts at Sichuan Agricultural University, a school that Jim had originally planned to visit during the week after the earthquake. I was earthquake-skittish but willing to go along. Jim reasoned that the post-quake area was one of the safest places to be, since stresses along the fault line had been released by the earthquake. He thought it would take a long time to build up that amount of stress again.

Though we couldn't help with medical relief or physical reconstruction, we might be able, through teaching, listening, and stories, to help some with psychological recovery in the quake's aftermath. At the same time, we hoped to further heal ourselves and to deepen our understanding of China. In 2008, Sichuan Agricultural University had its main campus in Ya'an, about two hours' drive southwest of Chengdu along the same modern expressway that had been the final leg of Jim's earthquake evacuation route in May.

The town of Ya'an lines both banks of the Qingli River, a glacier-fed stream that runs down from the foothills of the Tibetan plateau toward the Chengdu plain. In previous times the town was a way-station for travelers venturing toward Tibet, as well as a center for crafting high-quality shoes. During our year of teaching there, it was not yet subject to much of the air and water pollution that plagued larger urban areas. Ya'an was generally a pleasant and green town. Among cities of its size in Sichuan, it was also known as the "rain city."

12

Post-Traumatic Recovery, the Ya'an Year

灾后重建。

"*The empire province of Szechuan, with the great navigable tributaries of the Yangtze . . . is about the area of France, . . . has a population estimated at (between 50 and 70 million), . . . has a superb climate ranging from the temperate to the subtropical; a rich soil, much of which, under careful cultivation, yields three and even four crops annually of most things that can be grown.*"

Isabella Bird, *The Yangtze Valley and Beyond*, 1899.

The school year 2008-2009, when I was a foreign English teacher at Sichuan Agricultural University in Ya'an, Sichuan, was not perfect—nostalgia has softened some of its less appealing aspects. However, there were times during this healing school year when I felt I was in the right place at the right time, doing the right things with the right people for the right reasons.

In autumn 2008, faculty, students, and support staff at SAU were still in the initial stages of recovery from the devastating May 2008 earthquake that had ended or shaken so many lives. The glory of the Beijing Olympics that August had softened the tragedy's edges a little, but there were still cracks in some of the campus buildings, still cracks in the lives of some members of the SAU community who'd lost property, friends, and/or loved ones in their hometowns. Schools and buildings throughout the region had been damaged or destroyed. Entire villages had been leveled. Nearly 90,000 people had been killed or were missing, with several million rendered homeless. Though there had been only two quake-related fatalities in Ya'an itself, many in the SAU student body and staff came from parts of Sichuan that had been badly affected. Jim and I were both still a bit shaky ourselves.

When we landed in Chengdu in early September, a few days after the start of the semester, SAU's Foreign Affairs Officer, Ms. Chen, was waiting for our flight's arrival. A ride down the Cheng-Yan expressway in a chauffeured school car brought us to the outskirts of Ya'an on a Sunday evening just before nightfall. A fine mist was falling. We passed a large factory with a stylized drawing of a panda on its smokestack. Nearby was a statue of a rearing horse, along with some Chinese signage we could not read. After a trip through more streets than existed in all of Ala'er, Xinjiang, we arrived at the SAU Foreign Teachers' Guest House.

Ms. Chen briefly introduced us to our landlady, Ms. Wang, and then she explained in English, "Tomorrow morning you eat here in the first floor dining room. I have bought bread. There will be boiled water for tea. Your first classes will not start until 10, so you should have time to eat and then prepare your lessons. Later, one of the other foreign teachers will help you shop for food. After that, you can prepare your meals in your apartment kitchen." Ms. Chen then left us with our landlady.

Ms. Wang did not speak much English, but used gestures to direct us and help us get settled into our second-floor apartment. She supplied us with bed linens, towels, a thermos of boiled water, and a set of apartment keys. Then she too left. We soon found our pajamas and prepared for sleep and the beginnings of our adjustment to altered time zones and cultures.

Shortly before our trip, Jim and I had discussed our respective teaching preferences—one foreign teacher was needed to specialize in teaching writing to sophomore English majors; another would tutor students in listening and speaking in preparation for TOEFL tests.

"I'd like to teach writing," I volunteered. "I know that's likely to involve grading papers, but I really enjoy both reading and writing. You're better at storytelling. Why don't you take the TOEFL students?"

Jim agreed, thinking he'd gotten the easier assignment.

The prospect of dealing with the writing classes pleased me. I'd been an inveterate scribbler ever since I first learned to form my letters. I felt confident I could help sophomore English majors improve their written English. I also thought that reading their essays and stories would give me added chances to learn about China and Chinese youth. In contrast with previous China teaching assignments, this year I would be expected to perform all the "standard" teacher activities—assigning homework, administering mid-term tests and final exams, taking class attendance, giving student grades. I would meet with classes for fifteen weeks of each twenty-week semester.

During the first term, my classes met on Monday, Tuesday, and Thursday mornings for two hours, including a short intermediate break. The three equally sized groups totaled sixteen young men and sixty-five young women in all. Each section had a different group personality. Monday's group was studious, serious, even a bit stuffy. Tuesday's class was more free-wheeling, if sometimes lackadaisical or hesitant to participate. Thursday's students worked together best and also seemed the most interested in being helpful—they helped me understand the Chinese-only class lists I'd received. They also gave me the crutch of using names more familiar to my American ears: many had already chosen a "Mary," "Harry," or "Sue." For the others, I hurriedly composed a list of fairly standard English first names to choose from.

At the first meeting of each class section, I told the story of Jim's firsthand and my secondhand earthquake trauma and then stopped and wrote out Rick's email on the chalkboard:

"Dear Madam, Excuse please bad English. Husband and friends safe. Yours, Rick."

I told the students: "This message was SO important to me. Do you think I cared whether the grammar was totally correct?" I encouraged them to focus on content. The form of their compositions would be secondary.

As I worked to establish a classroom routine, I assigned short writing exercises in class, then a longer one as homework. That first week, I gave the students three options for a homework theme: the earthquake and its aftermath; the Olympics; or the Paralympics, for competitors with physical disabilities, being held in Beijing that September. Nearly everyone chose to write about the Olympics. My probing about the earthquake had been seriously premature and inappropriate. Months later, after students and staff had gotten to know me better, a few gave inklings of what the quake was like for them.

"My cousin was a primary teacher," one confided. "She was crushed while trying to move her students to safety."

"I was asleep in my SAU dorm room," explained another. "I thought at first that a bomb had gone off. I ran outside and tried to find a classmate who could tell me what had happened."

Although my classes focused primarily on writing, sometimes in class or at formal and informal campus gatherings, we just talked. Students occasionally confided other quandaries or hurts—a closeted gay friend, a relative with a gambling addiction, a classmate with alcohol problems. Reticence reigned in most interactions, but toward the end of the year, a few broached even more sensitive issues—grandparents who'd died during famines in the late 1950s and the torture of family members during the Cultural Revolution of the 1960s and '70s. Sometimes I felt that part of my role as a foreigner included being a safe repository for concerns that might provoke unwanted consequences if confided to a Chinese friend or colleague. In some of its excesses, the People's Republic had turned out not to be totally different from earlier emperors who'd obliterated whole families.

From time to time, I got a student's permission to read aloud in class an especially meaningful essay. I was touched when a student turned in a deeply felt piece, whatever its spelling or grammar flaws. Louisa completed her assignment about her best school experience by relating a story of her four-year-old self. Frustrated at being too young to accompany her older brother to primary school, she'd set up her own "classroom" on a large flat rock in her family's backyard. She alternated being teacher and pupil:
"Good morning, class."
"Good morning, teacher."
"Today we will practice the character 'da' (big)."
Louisa would carefully trace her "characters" onto the rock's surface, only interrupting her studies when called in for lunch. Now, as a college sophomore, she thought she might become a teacher once her schooling was complete, but long years of tests and rote learning had worn down her enthusiasm for formal education. She yearned to recapture the excitement she'd felt when she first discovered "school" as a four-year-old.

Theo, one of the tallest students and generally a star in pick-up basketball games, wrote a short persuasive essay about the practice of having an annual Sports Day at universities—he was vehemently against it. He thought such events detracted from study time without providing much physical benefit. Except for the physical education majors, students rarely took time to train before the springtime weekend event. The result: many competitors had to be treated for injuries or exhaustion. Some did not even finish their running races, throwing events, or high jumps. (Besides, the language majors always placed last.)

Several differences from our 2006-2007 Xinjiang teaching experience soon became evident: SAU was a larger, better established school, with a pedigree going back to 1906; it had nearly 2,000 graduate students along with 20,000 or so undergraduates; we were not the only foreign teachers. Even before we arrived, I'd gotten a welcoming email from Paul, who had already spent several years at SAU. Along with Irish-bred forestry expert Sean, French-born Paul gave us valuable, diplomatic advice about what to pack and how to interact with the school administration.

Sean had established and nurtured an active English Corner, held in a couple of covered pavilions near the school basketball courts on Thursday evenings. Paul arranged a Monday midday "Foreign teachers' lunch" at a small local snack bar. Most Mondays, we ate together, swapped ideas and honed our lesson plans.

"Why do we have to teach next Saturday?" I inquired soon after we'd arrived.

"This weekend was mid-autumn festival," Paul explained. "Some students wanted to go home to be with their families. The school tried to accommodate them by allowing for a long weekend, then double-loading classes next weekend so we won't get behind schedule."

Though we didn't bond as closely with Chinese faculty members as we had in Ala'er, we welcomed chances to socialize and learn from the other foreign teachers. One early weekend, Paul and Sean took us to a local mahjongg parlor and tried to teach us the game.

Several of the students, too, including even non-English majors, went out of their way to spend time with us. Joe, a graduate student who served as an unofficial adjunct to the Foreign Affairs Office, logged lots of hours swapping stories as he tended our sometimes recalcitrant computer equipment. Rupert, a pharmacy major, invited us to his hometown over the National Day holiday in October and then took us on a day hike to Tiantai Mountain.

"We must get up very early to catch a bus to the park," Rupert told us. Somehow we managed. Once at Tiantai, we saw gaudy over-sized cloth representations of the fireflies that frequented the area on summer evenings. Away from the main tourist area, we also got to see some as-yet-clear streams that later would merge to form Sichuan's major waterways.

Ying, a business major, arranged a more local hike up "Fortune Teller Mountain," the tallest peak in our immediate area. She recruited a set of hefty guys who came along to help if needed.

"Careful, Teacher," one of them cautioned as we mounted a steep slope inlaid with sandstone steps, "next step is wet. Please, let me assist you."

After a lot more wet steps up rough sandstone blocks with no railing, another of the guys took out his pocket knife and cut me a walking stick from a small tree growing beside the path. Partway up, we rested at a picnic area with tables and benches. I was getting tired. I was ready to beg off and stay where I was while the others went ahead. Just then a bouncy young Chinese girl wearing a frilly outfit and patent leather strapped shoes came uphill toward us, carrying her small dog in her arms. She stopped briefly and looked at me:

"Hello," she trilled in English. "Nice to meet you!" Then she skipped further up the path.

Tired or not, I was not to be outdone by an English-speaking Chinese little girl and her pet dog. The second part of the trail was easier. The view from the top was well worth the climb. Near the end of the trail was a small Buddhist monastery. Local monks served inexpensive vegetarian lunches to hikers as a way to earn money. They seated us at long wooden trestle tables in a bamboo-roofed enclosure. Each meal consisted of rice, plus some simple vegetable, sprouts, and tofu dishes. Before heading back down the mountain, we briefly explored a stone temple complex that had been badly damaged by the earthquake.

As the year unfolded, we made some in-town friends along with students and colleagues. The first to appear was Pearl, a young doctor at the local hospital who came fairly regularly to English Corner. On our first free weekend in Ya'an, Pearl arranged transportation and lunch at a nearby tourist town, "Shangli Ancient Town," a reconstruction of a typical 19th century farming community. Pearl wanted to improve her English and also was avid to show us the attractions of the area. Whenever all of us had free time during the week, she'd take us on afternoon visits to local parks and tea houses where we watched old ladies click their mahjongg tiles at lightning speed. One weekend she guided us on an over-a-mountain-pass trek to Hanyuan County, a fruit-growing region where she'd grown up.

If there was a silver lining to the earthquake's aftermath for the Ya'an area, it was the influx of large numbers of captive pandas to a panda research station nearby. During the disaster's immediate aftermath, most surviving pandas and staff from the badly damaged center at Wolong were relocated to Bifengxia, about ten miles from Ya'an. One autumn Saturday, Ms. Chen took the foreign teachers there for an outing.

A school van collected us at the foreign guesthouse just after eight. Our driver safely managed the short journey along the narrow twisting road to Bifengxia. The surrounding hillsides were covered in sub-tropical vegetation, with lots of bamboo thickets. The park, along with the ubiquitous kitsch and tourist trappings, also had an extensive set of panda enclosures. First, of course, we visited the pandas—nearly a dozen of various ages and temperaments.

"Now I'll show you the valley floor," Ms. Chen told us as she shepherded us to an outdoor elevator near the park entrance. We glided smoothly down nearly a hundred meters along a rock face to a trail that meandered along a small stream, through woods, and beside high cliffs. After maybe a quarter mile or so, Ms. Chen stopped in an open area and pointed up at several dark shapes about two-thirds of the way up one light gray cliff face.

"See those?" she asked, then elaborated, "Those are some of the famous 'hanging coffins' of this region. No one knows exactly how they got there, or why they were positioned the way they are. Scientists have dated them as several hundred years old, but none of the people who live here now know much about them."

We couldn't see them very well. The most distinct one looked a little like a small ebony piano frame that had been fastened to an especially steep part of the cliff side. The coffins seemed more puzzling than spooky. If they were made of wood, why hadn't they disintegrated in this damp climate? Why had the culture who left them disappeared? No one seemed even to know for sure where they had originated and how they had been transported to the cliffs. After squinting at them for a few minutes, we moved on.

Ms. Chen knew the trails by heart, arranging our wanderings so that we happened on snacks and lunch at convenient times. During spring festival that year, we showed off the park to our friend Jane Wang and her husband, back in the Chengdu area for the holidays.

Partway through the first term, Jim got permission from the school's foreign language coordinator to hold a weekly evening indoor and more formal English program with a bigger audience than the groups that typically showed up for English Corner. I sometimes helped around the edges, usually picking a song to share that had some relation to the week's topic. Jim's TOEFL students made excellent progress, and the English program gave him exposure to the wider student body.

I concentrated mostly on the sophomore English majors. As the skill level of my writing students improved, I tried to get them to do a short "Western-style" research paper as a term project. It would take six weeks, with intermediate drafts to be turned in along the way.

Deadlines in China are rarely hard and fast, I learned. Several of the students who typically did well on regular homework were floored when I reminded them, five weeks into this six-week assignment, that their final drafts were due the following week. I reiterated that I would deduct points from their grade progressively for each day the final paper was late.

"No, Teacher," they whimpered, "you wouldn't do that. I've been very busy with my other classes. Please may I have more time?"

Other students bridled when I commented on their intermediate drafts that they would receive failing grades if they continued to copy most of their wording verbatim from the internet.

"Why should I try to write in my own words," one student protested, "when someone with more fluent English than mine has already written about the same topic?" His approach had a certain logic to it, but missed the point of an original composition.

Subject matter proved a stumbling block with a few students. Initially, I offered no constraints on topics, except to emphasize that it was wise to find subjects that were "not too big, and not too small." Students would write a paper of 1500 to 2000 words. They would need to explore their topic without repetition, but with adequate coverage of the topic's main points. I asked each student to pick two or three possibilities for writing. Most chose subjects of a personal interest such as a Chinese writer or hero or some aspect of historic or contemporary Chinese culture that puzzled or fascinated them. It was usually easy to select the topics that had the strongest potential. However, a few students chose topics that seemed too broad, too narrow, or too controversial.

Peony, one of the best students in her section, wanted to write about some aspect of "democratization in Tibet." I suggested we meet privately to discuss how she wanted to handle this sensitive subject.

"What do you mean by democratization?" I asked her.

"I want to show how China has worked to give more voice to the oppressed peasants of this region, reducing the influence of the former feudal ruling class based in Buddhist monasteries," she told me.

"Do you know that Tibet and its people are viewed very differently in most Western countries from the view in official Chinese sources?" I ventured. "Is there maybe a different subject you'd like to research?"

Peony was adamant. She came from peasant stock and was a scholarship student at SAU. The plight of peasants in any part of the world was one she strongly identified with.

Her early drafts presented a far different slant on Tibetan society than what I'd been exposed to in American media. Tibet had been an economically backward region before the Chinese intervened; China had invested disproportionate sums to develop the transportation and economic infrastructure there, and now the majority of Tibet's people enjoyed vastly improved standards of living. Peony's drafts were well-written. However, the sources listed in her bibliography were all official Chinese publications. I suggested that she include at least one source from outside China, though it was sometimes difficult to access such sources in either written or internet form. I no longer have a copy of her final paper, in which she had toned down her earlier rhetoric and cited a Hong Kong based source.

As the first anniversary of the May 12, 2008, earthquake approached, Jim and I realized we each still had some healing to do. Jim hadn't yet been back to the site of his previous hike. I had a vague pre-quake impression of the worst impacted areas, based on our 2004 trip to Wolong, but I had yet to see any damage closer to the epicenter than Ya'an. On Tuesday, May 12, 2009, both of us were busy with class preparations and missed the evening candlelight memorial service some students and staff held on the central campus square.

The following weekend, though, the two of us were able to travel to parts of the area most affected by the earthquake. Our Chinese friend Sheila, who'd been hiking with Jim and American companion Jerry when the earthquake hit, had recently returned to China after a year of graduate study in the U.S. She arranged with a close friend to get the three of us a car and driver from Sichuan's capital city of Chengdu into the Wenchuan corridor, the area of worst destruction. It was not an officially sanctioned visit. Had we asked formal permission, it would likely have been denied. But the trip was very important for Sheila and for us. We were also able to see and to thank some of those who'd helped Jim, Jerry and Sheila both before and just after the quake.

Around midday, we arrived at Peach Blossom village and met the woman who had hosted the hikers the night before the quake. Her inn had been somewhat damaged, but was safe enough to stay in, so we arranged for lodging that night, along with supper and the next day's breakfast. Then we hiked up into the hills. After a couple of hours on a steep gravel track, we arrived at the home of the family who'd fed lunch to the three hikers the day before the earthquake. Jim had taken pictures of them the previous year, posing in front of their native stone rustic house.

They smiled warmly in welcome. With Sheila as translator, they invited us inside, offered us tea, and talked a little about how the quake had affected them.

"It was a scary time," the husband informed us. "We did not know at first if our granddaughter was safe at school. We were very happy when she got back home. Schools were closed for several weeks after that. I was kept busy helping neighbors whose houses had been more badly damaged than ours."

Then he switched topics slightly. "We are very happy to see you are alive and well. After the earthquake, we had no way of knowing if you had reached safety. Please stay for supper."

We politely declined, needing to return to our hostess in the village below. Before we left, though, Jim took several more pictures of this older couple and their young grandson. I especially remember the grandfather's rough workman's hands—he had constructed their house with help from neighbors, using only the most basic tools.

The following day, we saw the small village where the hikers had been sheltered for the rest of the afternoon after the 2:28 p.m. quake. There, too, our hosts were overjoyed to see that Jim and Sheila were alive and well, that they had not been killed during their later travels, when many roads were closed and others subject to unpredictable landslides. We were tickled to meet the baby granddaughter who'd survived the quake in utero.

Both villages we visited had extensive property damage—the first village had had a town gate with a carved goat head at its top. The gate had toppled and the goat head still lolled on the ground. At the second village, we heard for the first time the story of how villagers had been "saved by the cabbage truck."

Sheila again translated as a village elder elaborated.

"That Monday was the day we'd scheduled to harvest our cabbages and load them onto the produce truck to sell in Chengdu. To harvest the whole field and load the truck in a single day, we needed everyone's help. We had to work steadily. Even older people who could no longer bend to slice the cabbage heads brought drinking water to the fields."

"The truck arrived mid-morning. We'd only harvested about two-thirds of the field and were all busy at work when the earthquake struck. Any other day, we'd have been resting in our cool stone houses after lunch. If not for that cabbage truck, many of us might have been injured or killed. The cabbage field was the flattest land in the village, so once we'd finished the harvest, we could use it as a place to set up tents for temporary shelter. "

Mid-afternoon of our return trip to Chengdu, we stopped in Dujiangyan, one of the hardest hit larger cities. We shared a late restaurant lunch of noodles and vegetables with Sheila's cousin Rick, writer of the wonderful post-quake email. We could see a slight family resemblance. Rick downplayed the service he'd done us. He was still somewhat subdued. While Sheila and Jim made a quick visit to Sheila's parents, Rick took me in his small pickup for a brief tour of other parts of the recovering city.

"It was difficult time," he told me. "I pull many people and bodies from rubble. Some people I recognize—classmates, coworkers. Some families I can give hopeful news, say what hospital or clinic to visit. Others I must tell, 'Your son killed' or 'Your daughter killed.' Very sad."

On a later China visit I learned that for Rick, if there was one bright spot in the wake of the tragedy, it was the generosity of the U.S. National Basketball Association. With help from former Houston Rockets star Yao Ming, one of Dujiangyan's high schools would get a state-of-the-art indoor basketball complex, a big draw for young men in a China nearly as basketball-crazy as the USA.

In late May, we packed and repacked, graded papers and exams, made travel plans for our return to the U.S. A few days before our final evening English program, leaders of the school's English Club, which included both English majors and students from other fields, came to us.

"Teacher Jim and Teacher Jinny," they began. "We know you like to plan each week's English program. We have really benefited from your teaching. We would like to have half an hour at the end of this week's program to do a presentation of our own."

Surprised and flattered, we agreed. For the first part of the program, Jim retold one of his favorite narratives, a folk tale about two travelers:

A traveler came upon a bent old farmer working in his field. Eager to rest his feet, the wanderer said "hello" to the farmer, who seemed glad for a chance to straighten up and talk.

"What kind of people live in the next town?" the stranger asked.

"What were the people like where you've come from?" the farmer quizzed in turn.

"They were worthless. Troublemakers, lazy bums. They never helped each other out, and you couldn't trust any of them. I'm happy to be rid of them."

"Is that so?" replied the old farmer. "Well, I'm afraid that you'll find the same kind of folks in the next town."

Disappointed, the traveler trudged away, and the farmer returned to work. Sometime later, another stranger came by from the same direction and greeted the farmer. They stopped to talk.

"What sort of people live in the next town?" he asked.

"What were the people like in the town you've come from?" asked the farmer again.

"They were the best people in the world. Hardworking, honest, and friendly. I'm sorry to be leaving them."

"You're in luck," smiled the farmer. "You'll find the same kind of people in the next town."

Then the students took over. They'd assembled some of their favorite images of us from the year just ending and projected them on a large screen at the front of the auditorium. Rupert, the student they'd chosen as emcee, narrated them, then elicited testimonials. Different students came to the microphone to tell us, in well-rehearsed English, how much some of our activities and attitudes had meant to them. I don't remember their exact words. They were generous with their praise:

"Thank you for teaching us," was nearly universal.

"Thank you for showing us what love is," from a young lady whose boyfriend had befriended us.

"Thank you for your stories."

"Thank you for your songs."

"Thank you for going on long walks with us."

"Thank you for showing us how to make cookies and carrot cake."

"Thank you for listening to us."

"Thank you for caring."

Once the individual thank-yous were finished, about thirty of the students we knew best came up onto the stage and formed a sort of chorus line with us at its center. They linked arms and sang, karaoke style, while the alphabetic transcription to my favorite Chinese song scrolled by on the screen. Originating as a poem nearly a thousand years ago, the lyric tells the story of a young man who, after a night of drinking wine and gazing up at the full mid-autumn moon, mourns the absence of his brother.

"If only we could have stayed together to a ripe old age," he sighs. Surrounded by these special young people, realizing how much I'd relished our time together, thinking about our upcoming separation and how unlikely it was I'd meet most of them again, I choked up a little as I sang along.

13

For Richer, For Poorer

贫富悬殊。

"From the fire in his eyes, and the barely restrained fury in his voice, I honestly think that he is going to say 'ge ming.' Revolution.

But he doesn't.

'Ren shou,' he says, spitting the words out between his teeth. 'Endure. That is all we can do. Ren shou. We can and must endure. That is all we have ever been able to do.'

I stare at him and slowly shake my head. He has just summed up thousands of years of Chinese history. Endure is all that Old Hundred Names have ever been able to do. For all the progress in the wealthier parts of China, endure is all that hundreds of millions of common people in the poorer countryside and the western regions ever see themselves doing in future."

Rob Gifford, *China Road*, 2007.

In its preparations for the world exposition it hosted from May through October 2010, Shanghai pulled out all the stops to create the biggest, most successful fair ever. I arrived in China that year in late summer, traveling with Jim. We'd arranged to spend about ten days in Shanghai before heading back to Ya'an for short-term volunteer teaching assignments at Sichuan Agricultural University. We then hoped to travel in more rural parts of Sichuan. We'd used the internet from the U.S. to make advance Shanghai hotel reservations: a non-smoking room in a modestly priced guest house. Recommended by a former teaching colleague, the guest house was not far from the southwestern Shanghai apartment block where she now lived with her new husband and her recently widowed mother-in-law.

In the decade since we'd last visited Shanghai, the city had further punctured the sky with new office and apartment towers. It had built out huge quantities of housing, commercial space, and public infrastructure. Our guest house was a mid-rise building next door to a taller luxury hotel under the same management. The complex overlooked a major expressway interchange, a short block from the nearest subway station. Once we'd finished registration formalities, we settled into our comfortable room on the top floor. We had all the amenities dear to tourists from Western countries: a sit toilet, hot and cold running water, a thick but firm mattress, clean sheets, soft towels, even a special tap that dribbled out water safe for drinking. There was a small fridge, a small safe for valuables. After minimal unpacking, we fell into bed and went quickly to sleep.

I awoke early the following morning, a Monday, and watched the city awaken in turn. Motorized traffic thickened on the expressways below. Subways rumbled. Street vendors offered snacks. Shopkeepers began unlocking and rolling back the vertical metal shutters that secured their small stores at night. At the edge of my vision, under one of the expressway overpasses, several people rose, folded up their sleeping blankets, stowed them out of the lightly falling rain, and began the waking portion of their day. Jim and I soon grabbed a quick breakfast at a local fast food restaurant, then spent most of the day on foot exploring the urban neighborhoods closest by.

That evening, we went for supper to "Ikea Food," a cafeteria-style restaurant in the large Scandinavian discount home goods store across the highway interchange from our guest house. Threading our way among the whizzing vehicles to get there was daunting—we later found a usable underpass, frustrated that pedestrian access and bicycle lanes were so scarce and hard to find. At the restaurant, we got our trays, selected our food, and snagged a small, still-empty table. Lots of young Chinese couples or Chinese families with a baby or a small child sat at the tables around us, savoring Swedish meatballs and noodles at rock-bottom prices.

After a first couple of days to adjust my internal clock and to learn the rudiments of Shanghai's extensive subway system, I ventured to the Shanghai World Expo. "Better city, better life" was the theme and mantra of Expo 2010, the first fully global fair since 1992. My brief forays during three different days were a drop in the bucket of the 73,000,000 visits to the fair, a new record. I barely scratched the surface of the 246 national and organizational pavilions that made this the biggest of all global expositions, both in land area and in number of exhibitors.

On our first day at the fair, we spent part of our time at one of the "theme" pavilions. The English title was ambiguous: "Footprint."

"Do you suppose they'll ask us to take our shoes off?" I wondered out loud.

Picking our way through the exhibit, we finally figured out that we were seeing the "urban footprint" of progressive civilizations, all the way from the earliest Mesopotamian cities to modern metropolises and megalopolises. The exhibit wasn't crowded—I found it informative, but somewhat dry and uninspiring. It did represent the overall theme of the fair quite well, though—China was urbanizing rapidly. This Expo tried to point the way toward a better urban environment.

The overall design of the Expo site *was* inspiring, as were the exteriors of many of the national and organizational pavilions. The layout included lots of rest areas, eating areas, and open space. Motorized shuttles regularly whisked visitors around the huge site. At Expo entryways and at many of the larger exhibits, temperature-activated overhead misters cooled those waiting in lines in hot weather.

Because exhibits for major countries like China, the United States, England, France, Germany and Russia had prohibitively long queues, we stuck to the smaller countries. I enjoyed the Canada pavilion best. The design of its building incorporated high wooden walls and other natural materials. Canada also included a distinctive feature that minimized a problem plaguing other exhibits I walked through. At these other exhibits, pavilion volunteers fluent in Mandarin and English would be stationed at the entrance doors to the exhibits' main halls.

As crowds thickened, they'd explain in both languages: "The next show will start shortly. There will be room for everyone. Please stay in line. There's no need to crowd the doorways." Their pleas fell on deaf ears as eager patrons rushed and jostled each other to be first among the next group in. The Canada pavilion was an exception. Long curving corridors lined with pictures and animation emptied into a larger open area. I didn't even realize I'd arrived at a "main" part of the exhibit until its short presentation was over. Then exit doors swung open to let everyone out.

We interspersed our visits to the fair with visits to old friends in this mega-city, one of China's largest. We explored parts of both banks of the Huangpu River, which bisects Shanghai into "Shanghai Pudong" (east of the river) and "Shanghai Puxi" (west of the river). In advance of the fair, Shanghai had extensively upgraded and expanded its subway system, which now included thirteen highly automated lines, with signage in Chinese and English. Verbal announcements were repeated in Mandarin, English, and Shanghai dialect. The subway system's improvements would last long after the fair's closure, as would several of the large performance spaces. In most neighborhoods where we walked, streets and sidewalks showed evidence of recent repairs. During an evening visit with our former colleague Chelsea and her family, we learned that the large apartment complex where she lived had gotten a fresh coat of exterior paint just before the fair's opening. Eventually the buildings in Chelsea's complex would need another coat of paint, but for now they were bright as new.

Before we left Shanghai, we checked out its latest longer-distance transportation technologies. On a weekday excursion to the nearby city of Suzhou, the "Venice of China," we rocketed along via a high-speed bullet train that made the sixty-mile journey in just over half an hour. Even more impressive was the experimental "maglev" train line that linked one of the city's eastern subway stations with Pudong International Airport. We wanted to ride the train just to see what it was like. We took a digital picture of the maximum speed that the train reached on its eight-minute ride between city and the airport, nearly twenty miles away: 431 kilometers per hour (roughly 285 mph).

Through the maglev train windows, we got brief glimpses of the Chinese countryside and the small villages that still existed outside the urban core. Later in the autumn, after a short-term teaching stint in Ya'an, we'd get a more extended chance to view life in the countryside, along with the vast changes going on in China's less urbanized areas. While planning our 2010 trip, we'd emailed back and forth with our Ya'an friend Pearl. She suggested that we might be able to revisit her home county that fall. In early November 2010 as our short-term teaching assignment in Ya'an neared its end, Pearl came to English Corner one evening and laid out a plan. She would enlist the grandson of one of her elderly patients to drive us over the mountain to Hanyuan County for a long weekend. If administrators at the local high school were amenable, during the following week we might get a chance to teach sample lessons to high school English students at the big new public high school. Pearl would come with us for the first couple of days to help us get settled. After that, she'd need to return to the hospital in Ya'an to resume work. She'd be available via cell phone if we had any questions or needed her further assistance.

I was nervous. What if we had a traffic accident on the twisty mountain roads? What if we got into trouble with local authorities? What if we couldn't figure out how to contact Pearl's cell phone when we needed help? What if no one could understand our still-limited Chinese? What if, what if, what if? By the time Pearl brought a car and driver to the SAU Foreign Guest House on a misty Friday morning, I'd calmed a few of my inner demons. Jim and I stowed our travel bags in the trunk and got in. We settled back and prepared for the twists and turns of a mountainous ride we'd taken with Pearl once before, in late May 2009. That ride had involved different drivers, but the same general route. Pearl then had wanted us to get a glimpse of the area where she'd grown up. She'd also wanted us to meet some of the students in her former high school.

Spring can be a beautiful season in Sichuan. Along with the rain and the mist, there are clear periods when the fields and orchards practically glow with blossoms and new growth. By midmorning of the May Friday in 2009 when we first visited Hanyuan County, the mist had melted into a day of jewel-like clarity. We stopped briefly in a town that had formerly been a station along the tea-horse trade route of earlier centuries. We chewed down a pizza-like snack while examining samples of the pottery that is also an area specialty. Then we gassed up the car and climbed higher and higher into the hills. Near the highest pass, we stopped on the shoulder, gazing across a valley to snow-capped peaks in the distance. The summit of the highest peak, 25,000-foot Gongga Shan, was invisible, wreathed in clouds.

Descending the opposite side of the mountain, we saw slope after slope covered with cherry trees. At the higher elevations, they were still blossoming. In the valleys, they had set fruit, some of it for sale at local roadside stands. We spent the night in a small guest house beside a rushing river. Pearl dropped us off, made sure we had her cell phone number, then went off to visit her brother, promising to pick us up at eight the following morning to meet with local students. We arrived at their school gate by nine. Once inside, we were dismayed at the state of the campus. Hanyuan was further from the 2008 earthquake's epicenter than Ya'an, but a quirk in its geology made the shaking there almost as strong as in some towns much closer to the epicenter.

Classroom buildings had developed large cracks. Deemed unsafe, they had been abandoned. Adding to the school's challenges was the construction of a major hydroelectric dam several miles downstream. The area of the school, along with most of the town it was part of, would in a few months be inundated by the lake the dam would create. Rather than pour funds into construction of a short-lived replacement campus, the school was making do with temporary bamboo classrooms. We shared songs and stories with the students, then posed for pictures. Before we got back into our temporary car to head back to Ya'an, a few of the leading students cornered us.

"Please come back next year," they challenged. "Come visit our new school once Hanyuan City is rebuilt, up there." They pointed to the steep slope where we'd noticed a never-ending procession of trucks hauling rocks, debris, and building materials. This is where we were headed in November 2010.

The road was just as curvy as we remembered. During the autumn of 2010, spot shortages of diesel fuel had caused disruptions in long-haul trucking. Parts of our route were lined with trucks waiting to replenish their near-empty tanks at the few stations with available diesel. More than once, we narrowly avoided a collision when an overly aggressive car driver pulled out and tried to pass the gauntlet of trucks through not-quite-wide-enough openings. Soon enough, the hotshot got stymied. He then reversed, backing up toward the other cars that had piled up behind him. The same trip that had taken less than five hours in spring 2009 took nearly seven in autumn 2010, but our driver got us safely through.

When we got to Hanyuan City, the landscape was unrecognizable. The valley floor where most of the former city had nestled was now a lake. A small remaining settlement above the water line on its far slope was serviced by a ferry that went back and forth several times an hour. The relocated new city on the near shore was very steep, with frequent retaining walls. Landscaping of its major roadways was still in progress. Large trucks brought in nearly mature trees, which workers then carefully offloaded and lowered into tree wells beside the more level stretches. Once the trees were in place, a different landscape worker tamped down the earth around each tree, then pruned the tree back to its core and attached an IV drip bag.

"What's he doing?" we asked Pearl.

"The IV bags are filled with nutrients for the new trees," she explained. "A little like a tree intensive care unit," she chuckled. "Pruning, then feeding the trees this way lessens the shock of being transplanted. It helps them survive until they grow strong enough to make it on their own."

When we arrived at the high school for our pre-arranged visit, we recognized hardly any students, though a few said hello. One of them even remembered having seen us during his year of temporary bamboo classrooms. The replacement complex was impressive—a peach-and-orange cluster of concrete and stucco perched above the main street of the town. A few level playing fields had been gouged out of the hillside. Stairs were superabundant. The school, built for a capacity of several thousand middle schoolers, was not yet half full. With Pearl and the friend who'd kindly lent us a guest room in her new apartment, we wandered the new city's nascent commercial district. Parts of the city were receiving power from the new dam, but the majority of the generated electricity traveled via high-tension lines over the pass toward Chengdu and other, more urban parts of the power grid.

Our jaunt to Hanyuan County ended with a six-hour bus ride to Chengdu, where we visited briefly with Jane Wang, now returned from Xinjiang and in the process of taking graduate courses in linguistics. Jane worried about inflation, about rising housing prices, about her husband's extended absences—he was still teaching in Xinjiang and only made it back to Sichuan for long holidays. Jane and Meng had become part of China's rising middle class, among an increasing number of "DINK" (double income, no kids) couples in China's young adult generation.

Rather than take the most direct route from Chengdu back to Shanghai and then the U.S., we'd pieced out an end-of-trip itinerary that would include visits to another rural area, in one of China's poorest provinces, Guizhou, and then to one of its wealthiest and most technically advanced cities, Hangzhou.

Earlier in the year, an American friend had introduced us to Ms. Li, a visiting Chinese teacher from the small city of Kaili, home to many ethnic minority Miao. We still had vague designs on further long-term teaching assignments. Perhaps Ms. Li might provide an entree at a Kaili high school. A teaching future in Guizhou did not materialize, but we were able to arrange some touring of outlying area villages courtesy of the school. The misty landscapes reminded me a little of Ya'an. Local women wore colorful aproned costumes and peaked caps. Many houses were made of wood. Our longest trek took us over a low mountain pass to "Thousand Household Village," a Miao tourist spot whose inhabitants seemed to be mostly older. One younger man, a former student of Ms. Li, showed us around his housing compound.

"We heat mostly by wood," he told us. "Because our houses are wood, too, there's high fire danger. With government's help, we work to install water pipes, help reduce fire danger."

China's rapid economic rise has created the largest middle class of any nation. It has also created several hundred billionaires. A 2015 Forbes wealth index listed some Chinese as young as their mid-thirties with assets in U.S. dollar equivalents of at least one billion. High on the wealth list is Jack Ma, a fifty-something Hangzhou resident who founded internet marketing giant Alibaba.

When we visited Hangzhou, in late November 2010, we rented a small, windowless room in a modestly priced tourist hotel close to Hangzhou's scenic West Lake. I spent as little time in the hotel as possible, preferring to wander the surrounding business districts and nearby parks. As Jim and I strolled along one particularly opulent block, I did a double take.

"Is that a Maserati dealership?"

"Looks like it. Maybe the proletariat shops next door, at the Ferrari showroom," he deadpanned.

"While the old wealth heads down the block to check out the Rolls Royces," I shot back.

"I wonder what kind of car Mr. Ma drives."

Over the course of the years when I've traveled in China, overall living standards have improved tremendously. The "most wanteds" list that in the 1950s might have included such basics as a bicycle, a radio, and manufactured shoes, more recently had moved up to washing machine, mobile phone, television, computer, air conditioner. Many of China's burgeoning urban middle class now have private motorized transportation, either motorcycles or cars. The statistical poverty rate throughout China decreased from 81 percent in 1981 to only a third as high, 27 percent, by 2012. However, there are pockets that the new affluence has largely passed by. No one seems to know how to improve the lives of families in rural areas and in small cities like Hanyuan and Kaili. An estimated 300 million Chinese, nearly the entire population of the U.S., have left the countryside to search for work in China's major cities. Some are probably homeless, like the few underpass squatters I noticed on our first day in Shanghai.

Areas like the region around Kaili and near Pearl's hometown were struggling. Though infrastructure for the replacement Hanyuan City was impressive, lots of fertile bottomland had disappeared under the new dam's lake. Thousands of people had been displaced. As a friend of Pearl's showed us around her newer, more spacious, more modern apartment, she freely admitted that she missed her former family compound. Houses and fields alike now lay several meters below the surface of the lake.

"Most of all," she told us, "I miss my garden."

14

Undrinkable Water,
Unbreathable Air, Untillable Soil

穹顶之下，山河失色。

"Why should we tolerate a diet of weak poisons, a home in insipid surroundings, a circle of acquaintances who are not quite our enemies, the noise of motors with just enough relief to prevent insanity? Who would want to live in a world which is just not quite fatal?"

Rachel Carson, *Silent Spring*, 1962.

"Already on the way home from the hospital, I started to worry. The smell of black smoke and burning fire was everywhere. I covered (my small daughter's) nose with my handkerchief. I know it seems stupid, since in her struggle to breathe through it, she'd inhale more smog. Before that moment, I'd never been afraid of air pollution, never even wore a mask. But now, there is a little life in your arms, her breathing, drinking, eating, everything is on your shoulders. That's when you begin to feel afraid."

Chai Jing, from *Under the Dome*, an online air pollution documentary posted in China in early 2015.

Instructions for my first trip to China in 1980 turned out to be of mixed usefulness:

"Take plenty of your own toilet paper," counseled one early piece of advice.

It's a good idea to have lots of anti-diarrhea medicine," proclaimed another.

"Whatever you do, don't drink the tap water!" cautioned a third. Once I actually got to China, I found that the upscale tourist accommodations our group spent time in had plenty of toilet paper, even if some of it at that stage wasn't Charmin soft. It turned out that I didn't need anti-diarrhea medicines, either—what I needed instead were some of the bran flakes my roommate Maria had brought after I got constipated from a steady diet of rich, fatty banquets.

However, the third caution was right on target—our hotel rooms were furnished with thermoses of boiled water, and our Chinese hosts impressed on us that we should use only the water from the thermoses, maybe even for brushing our teeth, because tap water was likely to contain bacteria and other disease-causing substances. On subsequent trips, I've continued to be cautioned about drinking water, though the amenities for travelers have changed. Now instead of refillable thermoses of boiled water, we're more likely to be furnished water in disposable plastic bottles.

As part of China's economic development, many streams became contaminated with heavy metals—contaminants that just boiling could not remove. The bottled water industry has become big business in China, with China overtaking the United States as the world's largest bottled water market in 2014. A Chinese Ministry of Water Resources report released in 2016 estimated that over 80 percent of China's shallow groundwater was unfit for drinking or daily use because it suffered heavy contamination from surface water discharged by industrial plants and farming units. All over China, potable water is increasingly scarce and expensive.

My direct evidence for poor water quality in China is spotty and anecdotal. In Guizhou near Kaili, I noticed a small stream that ran orange. When I asked our guide why, he explained that the discoloration came from a nearby mining operation. During an earlier visit to the small town where Huang had grown up in rural Guangxi, I noticed that the stream running under a pedestrian bridge through the center of town was murky and overgrown with vegetation. Huang told us that as a boy he'd fished and gone swimming in this stream. Back then, the water was clear. Sunshine occasionally glinted through the dappled shade of streamside trees, reflecting off the sand and small pebbles on the stream's bottom.

Now, one person was still trying to fish along a bank whose exact edge was nearly impossible to see. He was using an electric prod to stun any remaining fish, a practice Huang told us was illegal. I guessed that the fisherman might need the protein to help feed his family. I thought how sad it was that any food taken from this stream in rural China was likely contaminated.

Then I remembered warnings posted all along the banks of a small lake near my North Carolina home—any fish caught in the lake are likely to contain toxic chemicals called PCBs. People are cautioned not to consume more than one of these fish a month. I recalled, too, how in 2014 an electric utility in North Carolina dumped nearly 39,000 tons of coal ash from a poorly maintained holding pond into a local river, contaminating ground water over a wide area. Recent U.S. headlines have spotlighted large-scale drinking water contamination in cities like Charleston, West Virginia, and Flint, Michigan. More and more of our streams, rivers, lakes, and reservoirs also suffer from industrial and agricultural run-off.

When I first went to China, air pollution did not seem to be a big problem. China was still primarily an agrarian society, one where pollution from burning farm fields was fairly predictable, seasonal, and localized. My first trip occurred in summer, when there was no need for heating, when few buildings had air conditioning, and when private car ownership was rare. Heavily industrialized areas were typically off the tourist track, so received little notice from international visitors. Conditions in China have changed, big time. By 2010, private car ownership had soared, while improvements in road infrastructure struggled to keep up. One horrendous traffic snarl occurred in August that year, when a traffic jam including both trucks and cars stretched north of Beijing for more than 62 miles and took nine days to clear.

For many years, urban air quality declined. In December 2015, December 2016, and again in January 2017, air pollution in Beijing and other major northeastern cities reached such dangerous levels that schools were closed and automobile traffic severely restricted.

One wake-up call about Chinese air pollution came from former state television reporter Chai Jing. In 2015, she caused a stir with an online documentary about air pollution problems, both in China and elsewhere. Her film, titled in English "Under the Dome," was viewed over a hundred million times in China after its initial internet release before it was shut down a week or so later by government censors. Focusing mostly on China, the film also provided historical context from other parts of the world such as Britain's "killer smog" of 1952 (four days of heavy air pollution in December that caused an estimated 12,000 deaths) and Los Angeles's smog problems and its ongoing efforts to reduce vehicle emissions. Chai has said she produced her documentary out of concern for her young daughter, who was diagnosed in utero with a benign brain tumor that may have been caused by air pollution. Shortly after birth, Chai's daughter was successfully operated on—the tumor was removed. But the experience changed Chai's perspective.

The time when I most noticed air pollution in China was during our cross-country train trip on the way to Ala'er in August 2006. A government official we talked with then said that China needed to build its electric generating capacity quickly to continue fueling its expanding economy. Ramping up generating capacity came mainly from opening an average of one new coal-fired power plant per week.

All the way from Beijing to Xi'an, over six hundred miles, we rarely saw the sun, only a sky so murky we couldn't tell whether or not there were clouds. When I thought about it, I realized that much of the problem lay in our choice of travel mode—we'd been chugging along the same corridor as the freight trains that supplied the coal-fired power plants lining our route in China's densely populated east. We had pretty much been following the smog.

Ala'er's air was generally cleaner, and like many places in China, pollution tended to get worse during the winter months, when many municipal heating systems still ran on coal. During an English Corner Q&A session one chilly evening, I was waxing smug about America's superior ecological consciousness. I gave a scathing assessment of China's visibly polluted air. After a beat, Jane snapped back at me:

"Your country spewed great plumes and spurts of toxic chemicals into the air and water for over a century before you began efforts to clean up your dirty industries. What right do you have to criticize us when we're still just getting started on our economic development?"

She had a point. China has since shifted much of its emphasis for generating electricity from coal to renewable resources and nuclear facilities. During the first half of 2017, China reported that seventy percent of its new capacity was from water, wind, and solar facilities, two percent from nuclear, and only twenty-eight percent from fossil fuels. Still, because of existing capacity, about three-fourths of China's electricity is generated by coal-fired plants.

Though much of my time in China has been at agricultural universities, I am not a farmer. What I know about soil depletion comes from limited personal observation, or secondhand from what students and colleagues have told me and from official statistics. In 2014, China's official news agency Xinhua estimated that about forty percent of China's arable land was degraded:

"Degraded land typically includes soil suffering from reduced fertility, erosion, changes in acidity and the effects of climate change as well as damage from pollutants."

I've seen erosion wearing deep gullies into hillsides in the Loess Plateau, a region of silty soils along parts of the Yellow River that saw some of China's earliest settlements. Loess (from a German term for "loose") was described in a 2000 study as "the most erodible soil on earth." Deposited by windstorms over thousands of years, the loess is both fertile and easily degraded. During our cross-country train ride in 2006, I saw entrance doorways to loess cave dwellings in hillsides near Zhengzhou, but also more and more gullies. When in 2002 I visited downriver sections of the Yellow River near Zhengzhou, I noticed that centuries of silt buildup had lifted the river bottom above the level of surrounding land. Because of protective levees and extensive irrigation use, the river's water level was well contained, but a huge area had the potential for serious flooding. An extensive man-made flood had occurred in the region in 1938, when Nationalist forces tried to slow the advance of Japanese invaders by dynamiting a section of dikes near Zhengzhou. The water rushed out, flooding parts of three provinces, killing hundreds of thousands of peasants, and altering the river's course further east.

Few of the students I encountered either at Tarim University or at Sichuan Agricultural planned to engage in farming after graduation, whatever their training. On excursions from Tarim into the desert near Ala'er, I noted that groves of variegated leaf poplar trees were being cut down to make way for further cotton fields or residential building, leaving fewer trees to hold the soil or provide windbreaks during spring dust storms.

"That's too bad," Mao told me, "but I guess it's part of the price of progress." I wondered of any of Abdul's lessons in tree protection could have helped save these beautiful and beneficial poplars.

In Ya'an, the hillsides surrounding our campus contained small agricultural villages that drew students' interest only during peach blossom season. Then, they joined other tourists to revel in the springtime beauty.

As more and more Chinese adults leave the countryside in search of higher incomes and more comfortable lives in major cities, a knowledge base for good agricultural practices may erode along with the soil.

Comparative global statistics on arable land from 2005 indicate that China's acreage of farmable land (including pasture) was then a little over half that of the United States. When population differences are factored in, China's available per capita arable land is only about fourteen percent of America's.

China's economic resurgence in the late 20th and early 21st century has created increasing stresses on its overall environment as well as on its areas of natural beauty. Disasters, both natural and man-made, have taken an awful toll. The Wolong Panda Preserve was nearly wiped out during a 2008 earthquake; Jiuzhaigou National Park and surroundings suffered serious damage during a 7.0 quake in 2017. Air pollution has continued to be a problem, especially in northeastern cities like Beijing, Tianjin, and Shenyang, where unofficial sources in November 2015 registered a concentration of the small particles that can cause the most serious lung damage (PM 2.5) at over fifty times the World Health Organization's recommended safe level. During our recent brief 2017 stay in Beijing, we could access online air quality measures only intermittently, but the summer day when we spent time outdoors started with an early morning reading of 70 (moderate), and by midday had climbed to 152 (unhealthy for all groups).

Some of the same objections to environmental safeguards that get trotted out in the U.S. are potent in China as well: cleaning up dirty industries can be expensive; economic development is a top priority; restricting businesses' pollution makes them less competitive in the global economy. Over the past generation or so in China, there has been a countervailing increase in interest in ecological education and nature preservation, as the Chinese economy begins to mature and its pollution problems get harder to ignore. Since the first set of forty-four national parks in China was announced in 1982, both the number of parks and the land area set aside for natural areas has increased dramatically to 225 parks that make up nearly fifteen percent of China's overall land area. Efforts in China to rein in air and water pollution, to slow or reverse soil degradation, have had spotty results so far, though there have been some successes.

During my lifetime here in the U.S. it has often taken both acute and chronic instances of pollution to spur clean-up efforts. I remember winter days during childhood when our bedroom windowsills had thick layers of soot. Our closest river ran white with the run-off from nearby paper mills. The stink of fermenting mash from the whiskey distillery a couple of miles east of my house meant only that we were in for a rain or snow storm. When I was a young adult, a huge oil spill off the coast of California spurred an initial "Earth Day." Shortly thereafter, a cabinet-level Environmental Protection Agency was created within the U.S. government and charged with protecting the American environment, a charge it has struggled to fulfill.

No country is in a secure position to point fingers when it comes to responsible environmental stewardship. Along with its recent neglect of some of its natural surroundings, China has a lengthy history of blending nature and human activity.

15

Where the Wall Ends

不到长城非好汉。

"Something there is that doesn't love a wall, That wants it down."
Robert Frost, "Mending Wall,"
in *North of Boston*, 1914.

"There is no Planet B."
slogan on banners at the People's Climate March,
New York City, 2014.

In late spring 2017, Jim and I set out for China again, after a gap of nearly five years. In 2011-2012, we'd done one last unofficial teaching stint along China's southern coast. That experience, in a climate similar to Hainan Island's, mostly taught us that living full-time in a tropical paradise is different from vacationing there: tropical areas are subject to periodic tropical cyclones; in spring, temperatures warm and the humidity becomes oppressive.

Together, we roughed out a 2017 itinerary: we'd spend time partly with old friends, partly exploring by ourselves in areas new to us. This would be our first trip without any official "role"—we wouldn't be part of a tour group, nor would we be paid or volunteer workers. We were just two retirees with a hankering to see more of China. We'd fly to Chengdu and tour areas nearby with friends. Then we'd use China's extensive train system for further friend visits plus chances to explore both natural and man-made wonders. At the end of our trip, we'd stay briefly in Beijing, then fly back to America. The journey would turn out to be exhilarating, strenuous, and exhausting. Before we went, I hoped to get some sort of closure this time around—a way to tie together my previous array of visits and experiences with China. My stamina was declining, and I was not sure when, or even whether I'd have other chances to experience my "second home."

Our first stops were in Sichuan Province. We again got to see Jane, our former Xinjiang colleague. Jane was running a small private school in Chengdu for candidates for graduate school, providing tutoring in English and politics as preparation for the Chinese equivalent of the Graduate Record Exams. Her husband Meng had returned from Xinjiang, but was having trouble finding a permanent job due to his extended stay in a "terrorism suspect" area. We also visited one weekend with Pearl, the young doctor who'd come to English Corners in Ya'an and shown us around surrounding countryside. Pearl was switching from specializing in kidney conditions to working in a geriatrics program at a brand-new hospital on the outskirts of Ya'an. She was incorporating more empathetic approaches to the care of her patients, beyond just diagnosis and procedures. At the entry to her ward was a saying, printed in large script in both Chinese and English: "Cure sometimes, relieve often, comfort always." We got to observe a Saturday program of "clown doctoring" she'd initiated, modeled loosely on concepts championed by maverick U.S. physician "Patch" Adams.

Later in the trip, we visited with Maura, one of my former writing students who'd recently married. After undergraduate school, she'd gone on to get a master's degree in translation. Fully credentialed, Maura began work as an administrative assistant for a multi-national infant formula company with headquarters in Hangzhou, the capital city of her home province of Zhejiang. She helped us reserve a hotel room along the historic Grand Canal, near the southern end of a thousand-plus mile waterway that had been an early grain shipment artery. Still in use, the canal we could see out our hotel room window now carried passengers on "river buses," plus construction materials on an endless stream of barges. Maura waited until seeing us in person to share the news that she was expecting a baby. She and husband Xi were thrilled. They were working hard to get a new apartment furnished and ready before the baby came late in the year.

Our first venture northeast of Beijing took us to the coastal city of Qingdao. We arrived there by high-speed train from Hangzhou to spend a couple of days exploring the city. It hadn't been at the top of my list, but it was an easy train ride from Maura's current hometown and she had recommended it:

"I went there during my summer vacation when I was in graduate school. It's a pretty beach town. You might enjoy it."

I was curious about the evolution of this former treaty port that had been run by Germans from 1898 to 1914, then by Japanese until 1945. German-style architecture was evident at its historic main train station and in some of its downtown buildings. I drank an obligatory Tsingtao

Beer (brewed in what was then phoneticized as "Tsingtao" under the direction of its German colonizers starting in 1904). Together, Jim and I strolled parts of the city's seaside promenade, not that different from tourist meccas everywhere. One pretty day, we explored beaches further from town, including one that had hosted the sailing events for the Beijing Olympics.

Even further northeast, we explored parts of Heilongjiang, China's northernmost province. Heilongjiang gets its name from the "Black Dragon" river, which marks its boundary with Russian Siberia. The province shares both similar landscapes and a good bit of history with its northern neighbor. In its capital city, Harbin, we viewed Saint Sophia Church, whose exterior is a prime example of Russian Orthodox onion dome architecture. Its interior is no longer devoted to religion, but houses a somewhat run-down collection of poster-sized enlargements of photos of the city's history. We took a cable car across the Songhua River, a tributary of the Heilongjiang. In winter, its wide frozen expanse provides a backdrop for Harbin's famous Ice/Snow Sculpture Festival.

From Harbin, we took a slower train westward to Qiqihar, near Heilongjiang's provincial border with Inner Mongolia. Once there, we arranged a day visit to the Zhalong Nature Reserve, about an hour from town via taxi or bus. During peak bird migration season, Zhalong hosts up to six species of cranes plus many smaller migratory birds in its marshes and lakes. Birds along its flyway number in the tens of thousands. By the time we got there in late June, spring migration season had ended. Wild birds had traveled on to their summer quarters in parts of Siberia. We arrived at the park gate just after its morning opening and took a tram to the main viewing area. After wandering the park for most of an hour, seeing few birds, we reached an extensive wooden platform built on piers at one edge of a marshy area. A substantial crowd of humans was gathering, some with elaborate camera equipment.

"See cranes soon," a Chinese visitor explained to us, pointing to his watch. Several keepers carrying buckets appeared, followed shortly by a flock of perhaps fifty cranes, swooping over us in formation, then pulling up to land in the shallows nearby. We later learned that the heaviest of these cranes, weighing up to 25 pounds each, had spent

191

most of their morning in a large pen just out of sight beyond a small man-made hill.

Keepers dispensed ample quantities of fish. The birds enjoyed their lunch without seeming disturbed by the hundreds of tourists snapping pictures of them from a few yards away. Once the birds had eaten all the fish, the keepers used long bamboo switches to shoo the well-fed flock, now less inclined to fly, back to their enclosure until it was time for their next feeding.

At our next destination, Tongliao in Inner Mongolia, we discovered that we had again arrived in the "wrong" season—this time too early to get a glimpse of the Mongolian grasslands, which hadn't yet been coaxed into growth by summer rains. We did wander through the city's largest park, with a curving artificial lake full of families steering small paddle boats. At the lake's center was an island with a 100-foot high monument to Mongolian accomplishments.

We stayed in our most upscale hotel of the trip—a garden-style three-story edifice near the town's northern edge. Irrigated land bordered the hotel on two sides, mostly planted with flowers just starting to bloom. Along the edge of one flower field was what looked like a Dutch windmill—on closer approach, it proved to be a combination of snack bar, restrooms, and a small office. Behind our hotel was a larger office: a sales center for a luxury gated community still under construction. It advertised in Chinese and in English. A 10-foot billboard showed an evening patio gathering of elegantly dressed older adults with the caption, "Make your family proud." Some homes being promoted were in excess of 10,000 square feet.

After our most upscale hotel came our least comfortable train ride— ten hours on upper hard sleeper bunks to arrive at the city of Chengde in northern Hebei province. Chengde's main claim to fame was as the site of the former sumptuous summer retreat of Qing emperors fleeing the heat and humidity of Beijing. Because Chengde would complete our tour except for a brief stay in Beijing, we'd had limited flexibility in arranging our train schedule to get there. Seeing Chengde's palaces and gardens had been near the top of my "most wanted" list, but by the time we staggered off the train at 4 a.m., my ardor had waned considerably. I managed to get us a taxi to the hotel where we'd earlier reserved a room online. The building wasn't well lit, but the front entrance was open.

Jim walked up to the reception desk and rang the bell for service. By this time, neither of us had any Chinese phrases left. It took considerable effort just to stay upright.

A clerk in a somewhat rumpled uniform got up off the day bed behind the counter.

"We have a reservation," Jim told her, as she rubbed sleep from her eyes. "Batterson."

"Wait a moment," she responded. "Computer is slow. Passports, please."

Before either Jim or I fell asleep on our feet, she confirmed our reservation. With only a little delay, she managed to run our credit card, then gave us our room keys plus breakfast chits for the buffet in the hotel dining room later that morning. She pointed the way to the elevator, told us we'd be able to get our passports back after the hotel office opened at 8, then straightened her quilt, lay down, and went back to sleep. We took the elevator to the nineteenth floor and soon were asleep, too.

The hotel was a step down from Tongliao's luxury, but had the advantage of being almost next door to an entrance to Chengde Mountain Resort, the roughly rectangular two square mile park that had earlier provided emperors with relief from summer's heat. The palaces and gardens of Chengde took most of the 18th century to complete. The resort came to include depictions of landscapes from all over China, from the northernmost Mongolian grasslands to the fantastically shaped rock grottoes of China's southern reaches. Containing 72 scenic spots in all, with numerous man-made lakes and islands, the complex reached its apex under Emperor Qianlong. When completed in 1792, it included not only the original complex, but eight additional outlying temples, representing various religious traditions practiced by ethnic minorities in China.

Before we left the area, we took a bus to one of the outliers—a replica of Llasa's Potala Palace. Surrounded by a lesser wall, the compound had numerous gates and courtyards. Near the center of one large stone-paved area were several tall poles trailing ropes strung with prayer flags—a little like ship's rigging, or giant versions of the maypoles used in some Western springtime celebrations. I didn't see any monks, but the place had a sort of reverence all the same. It was as close as I was ever likely to get to the original in Llasa.

A final, shorter train ride brought us to Beijing, where we mostly stayed indoors in a hotel with a good air filtration system. During a brief foray to see the modern "temple" complex that had housed the 2008 Olympics, my eyes watered and my head ached—the subway ride back to the hotel couldn't come fast enough.

The Great Wall segment that met the ocean along a curving coastline partway between Qingdao and China's far north was not on a direct route to any of our other travel destinations, but I'd lobbied for this leg of the journey just as vehemently as Jim had insisted on seeing the natural wonders of Zhangjiajie's forest park. Seeing one of the eastern terminuses of the Great Wall *would* complete a series of sorts. I had first experienced the Great Wall near Beijing, then the Great Wall at its western extremity, and now I would view the Great Wall meeting the ocean in the east. I wanted to see firsthand where the wall jutted into the Bohai Gulf. Making it to both ends of this longest wall on earth was something not many tourists or travelers get to do. Before we took a taxi from our hotel to the park surrounding the wall itself, I tried to keep my expectations from galloping away with me. Jim politely expressed some interest.

After the taxi let us off near the park gate, I approached the ticket window with both our passports opened to the page that showed our pictures and our ages. Most of the other visitors we saw were Chinese, with only a smattering of foreigners like us. Many were in tour groups, but the park was not overly crowded on this pleasant day with a cooling ocean breeze.

"*Women shi lao ren* (we are seniors), *qi shi sui* (70 years old)," I told the ticket office clerk, pointing at our birth dates, hoping for the elders' discount that kicks in at age seventy at many Chinese parks. He motioned to a supervisor, who was quite generous to us foreign guests. The supervisor let us in free of charge.

When I later checked out the lavatories, I found that toilet facilities included icons and both Chinese and English signage about which toilet stalls were squat and which were sit—generally an indication that an attraction was frequented by international tourists.

Throughout the rest of the park, signage was trilingual—Chinese, English, and Russian. I learned that parts of the wall had been shelled by foreign powers during the Boxer Rebellion in 1900 and that there had been a pitched battle nearby in 1945 during the Chinese civil war. I walked to the wall's end and gazed out at the ocean. To my right was a sandy beach. To my left, a bit further away, a busy container port.

The wall's final abutment was stark, in contrast with the groves and flower beds that filled most landward areas of the park. About a mile of wall here at *Laolongtou* ("Old Dragon's Head") had been reconstructed during the 1980s and 1990s. The vicinity, including a couple of other refurbished wall segments further inland, was a popular attraction.

I was impressed by the scope and strength of the wall, but felt that the wall could not keep out anyone out who desperately, passionately wanted to get past it—a small boat under cover of night might suffice. Actually, forces of China's final imperial dynasty, the Qing, had come from north of the wall and marched south through a nearby strategic pass as the Ming Dynasty disintegrated due to corruption and infighting during the 17th century.

As glad as I was to have a chance to see the wall's section at Old Dragon's Head, I wasn't enlightened with any sense of closure. It was just a wall—a very big, very long wall that had sometimes kept invaders out.

Once I got back to North Carolina and resumed formalizing my impressions for this travel journal/memoir, I got increasingly frustrated. Trying to weave my experiences into any sort of coherent pattern was hard. I could rough out themes that have impacted modern American and Chinese societies equally, if in slightly different ways: urbanization and rural decline, increased material wealth unevenly distributed, aging human populations, environmental stresses, but how could I frame them into a meaningful conclusion? Would I ever fully understand my long-term fascination with China? Would I ever be able to help bridge the gaps in geography and culture that separated the U.S.A. and the P.R.C.?

At times during the sixty-plus years that I've been aware of the United States and mainland China, we've come up with similar partial solutions to common challenges despite our vastly different cultures and histories. At other times, what makes sense to Americans can be total anathema to Chinese, and vice versa, for reasons neither group entirely understands. I was missing any sort of closure. I doubted I'd ever understand China well; it was a little like trying to peel an onion that's growing new layers from the inside faster than outer layers can be cleared away.

After staring at my computer screen for far too long, I fell back on a coping mechanism that had helped clarify my thinking in the past: I went out for a walk. It was cloudy and cool. Just in case, I brought an umbrella. Before long, a fine misty rain began to fall.

I remembered the place in China where I'd experienced similar weather—the locale where I've spent the most time, the small Sichuanese city of Ya'an.

Ya'an lies where the foothills of the Tibetan plateau meet the edge of the Chengdu plain. Warmer and cooler air often mix. It rains a lot— nearly seventy inches in an average year, with some rain on at least 213 days. When I lived there, we often experienced what I called a "Ya'an rain." Not deluge, not downpour, not quite drizzle, neither mist nor fog, a Ya'an rain was a continuous showering of very fine droplets. Umbrella or not, a Ya'an rain spread enough humidity to steam up my glasses. I'd have to stop from time to time to wipe them off. A Ya'an rain was a meditative kind of weather, good for shifting my perspective slightly, not so much for making major readjustments.

Some afternoons, I'd take a break from grading papers or planning lessons to walk through SAU's experimental farm. The rain softened the landscape. I might follow a concrete ribbon, wide enough to accommodate a small tractor, through grain fields laid out on a barely noticeable incline. Other days I'd step off onto one of the person-wide paths between individual plots, or walk the road along back campus at the edge of the school orchard. Occasionally I'd stop to wipe my glasses, later keeping my eyes mostly on the walkway just in front of me.

Here in North Carolina, I debated putting up my umbrella. I looked down through slightly fogged lenses at the sidewalk, cracked in places due to ongoing construction traffic. As I walked along one of my favorite neighborhood circuits, I mused about a sense of closure. Why did I want my travels to fit into a neat pattern, anyway? Had this latest China trip just opened up new questions? Why had the Great Wall seemed both important and inadequate as a symbol for China?

I wondered whether to emphasize the role the wall's various sections had sometimes played as a deterrent to "barbarians," or instead to stress that parts of the wall had been breached multiple times, sometimes by opposing forces, at other times just by weathering and decay. I wondered if it was relevant to note that the Great Wall had not originally been continuous, but was cobbled together over long periods from shorter sections and spurs, some of which are still being rediscovered. I pondered the dual purpose of the fort at Jaiyuguan— it was not just a fortress but also a trading post, a stop along the Silk Road of caravans and goods traveling between Asia and Europe. My imagination turned toward other of humanity's previous attempts to wall out or wall in various invaders: animal species causing problems in U.S. waters and parks like zebra mussels or Burmese pythons; bacterial and viral infections like the Black Plague in medieval Europe; the global flu pandemic of 1918; more recent episodes of HIV/AIDS, SARS, Ebola, bird flu, swine flu, Zika.

I considered that in trying to create a narrative of manageable length from my experiences as an American fascinated with China, I'd probably left out relevant episodes and comparisons. What about the resurgence of bicycle use in relatively flat Chinese cities or the use of GPS and cell phone technology to provide networks of rental bike fleets? Why did I harp on air pollution in China's major cities but ignore the smoke and ash from massive U.S. forest fires that were casting a pall over some of America's urban areas, even over parts of sparsely settled Alaska?

Before I knew it, I'd nearly completed one of my favorite looping routes through our central North Carolina neighborhood—past the small businesses and professional building at our nearest corner, down a hill by an academic press's distribution center almost to a new apartment complex still under construction in our urbanizing town. Just short of the apartments, I turned right onto a meandering greenway trail that ended near one of the area's most expensive single-family home developments. Then I went past our neighborhood park, along a couple more slightly cracked walkways, and back to the entrance of our small, moderate-income condo complex.

I stopped for a second to wipe the moisture off my glasses before heading slowly back toward my current home. As the lightest of light rains continued to fall, my steps were a little lighter, too.

I realized that the effort of crafting this memoir had given me chances to reopen and reconsider my past experiences with China. As neither diplomat, journalist, nor business executive, I was unlikely to have a big policy impact on U.S.-China relations. As an individual citizen, though, I could retell my deepening understanding of China with skill and care. China had become a part of who I was. The weather had brought me a gift more important than closure. This gentle rain had brought me back in imagination to other misty afternoons a decade or so ago when I walked in Ya'an, half a planet away, breathed in clean air, and also felt at home.

Acknowledgments

Though the actual process of writing is a solitary enterprise, no book ever gets completed without input and assistance from many quarters. It would take pages and pages to acknowledge by name everyone who helped bring this book to fruition, and I'm sure I would leave someone important out. Instead, I'm going to try to thank groups of folks who helped me along the way. First, the pioneers and peacemakers of Servas and of the U.S. China People's Friendship Association who helped make my early visits to China possible. Second, my gratitude to members of various writing groups I've been part of over the course of decades. They've provided valuable critiques, and at the same time encouraged me to keep writing.

Thank you to the many China-interested friends in the U.S. who shared insights with me; thanks to the many friends and acquaintances in China who let me glimpse pieces of their lives. Thank you to readers and editors of this manuscript's succeeding versions who bore with me, making valuable improvements to the look and readability of the text. Thank you to the other writers in my biological and intentional families who've provided role models and inspiration. Thanks to the professionals who helped turn a rough manuscript into a publishable book.

There's one individual whom I will need to call out by name: my husband Jim Batterson. Through many years, Jim has found ways to prod and goad me into adventures I would never have embarked on, left to my own devices. Both of us are now officially "retirees," but Jim refuses to let my inner adventurer retire completely.

photo by Jim Batterson

About the Author

Jinny Batterson has spent nearly three years of intermittent travel and teaching in various parts of the People's Republic of China. Though she has spent much of her life on the U.S. East Coast, she has visited all fifty U.S. states, plus nearly thirty countries in the Americas, Europe, Africa, Asia, and Oceania. Her writings have appeared in Richmond, Virginia's *Style Weekly*, in *Carolina Woman*, and in various specialized publications. She continues to travel and to work at improving her word craft. When not on a plane, train, or bus somewhere exotic, she shares a small condo in central North Carolina with her husband Jim, numerous houseplants, and a low-maintenance "pet"—a ceramic cat.

CPSIA information can be obtained
at www.ICGtesting.com
Printed in the USA
LVOW13s2121080418
572726LV00001B/1/P